# "Life is a Jungle!"

## RON SNELL

Book Two of the Rani Adventures

the Rani
Adventures

# DEDICATION

If I had to pick just two people outside my family who defined my high school years, who stretched my wings and broadened my interests, who counseled and consoled during times of crisis, who gave me a way to learn and grow, those two people would be Uncle Jim and Aunt Anita Price.

They were my "dad" and "mom" in the children's home and to their credit, those who didn't get to live in the children's home a few months out of every year envied those of us who did. You will find their names often in the pages of my life.

I dedicate this book to you, Aunt Anita, with my gratitude and love, and to the memory of Uncle Jim, my hero and role model still.

# ACKNOWLEDGEMENTS

I wish I could just cut and paste the acknowledgements from my last book into this one. Unfortunately my mom, Editor Supreme, abandoned me halfway through to go back to Peru with my dad. My brother Terry said if I wasn't going to get it right he didn't want any credit. I think Sandy and Melody want to write their own books just to get even, and my dad's memories are so outrageous I couldn't include much of his input with a clear conscience. No matter what you think, I still do have a conscience.

That doesn't leave many people to acknowledge, or to blame. Marti Hefley once again tactfully dragged me kicking and screaming through the editing process, and Cyndi Allison did a great job of polishing Josh Barkey's cover ideas. And my mother *did* leave me access to a ton of her old journals, letters and photos, plus an e-mail address that sometimes worked.

I should also acknowledge Vivian Ginty's special help. She called to say that if I got this book done in time, she'd order a couple thousand copies. That provided exactly the kind of motivation that I needed, and I doubt that I would ever have finished without her encouragement. In other words, blame her.

My heartfelt thanks to those who read Book One of the Rani Adventures and let me know how much you enjoyed it and how stupid you thought we all were. This book, I'm afraid, may prove you right.

# Table of Contents

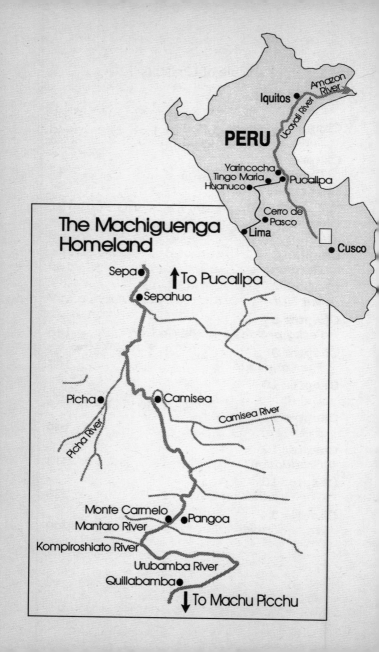

The Machiguenga Homeland

Sepa

To Pucallpa

Sepahua

Picha

Camisea

Picha River

Camisea River

Monte Carmelo

Pangoa

Mantaro River

Kompiroshiato River

Urubamba River

Quillabamba

To Machu Picchu

PERU

Iquitos

Amazon River

Ucayali River

Yarincocha

Tingo Maria

Pucallpa

Huanuco

Cerro de Pasco

Lima

Cusco

"What else did you get to do when you were growing up," asked a little friend, twisting her blonde hair with her index finger.

"Well..." I answered, "lots of things."

"Like what?"

"Like...well...if you'll sit really still on my lap, I'll tell you and everyone else can listen too."

My mind wandered back to a very different world as I talked. Sometimes we laughed so hard tears tumbled down our cheeks. Other times the pain washed over me like a crashing wave. But when I was done, when we each went home to bed, I thought all over again how fortunate I'd been.

# Chapter 1

## *Furlough*

I lay huddled in a torn yellow blanket, soaking wet from the rain dripping through the cane shelter where we camped on damp sand. My 12-year-old brother Terry, a year older than me, was asleep, though I didn't know how he managed. Wind blasted through the jungle, shaking enormous trees. Lightning sliced through the darkness, thunder crashed like cosmic drums and the river roared beside us. I wished desperately that the Machiguenga Indians we were with would get up, that the sun would come up, that the air would warm up.

Suddenly Miguel, whom we called "Grandpa," leaped to his feet and headed for his canoe.

"The river is rising," I heard him mumble to his wife. She grabbed their little boy and followed him without a word.

"Terry," I shouted, shaking his leg. "The river is coming up and the Indians are leaving." He was groggy and confused. By the time we'd collected our wits and hobbled to the gravel beach, the Indians were gone.

"They'll come back," Terry said confidently. "They would never leave us. They never have before."

"Yeah, but they've never taken off in the dark before either. I wonder where they went." We walked back to our flimsy shelter, tripping over rocks, and waited alone for the gray dawn.

Terry was dozing again when I noticed a black shape coming out of the jungle toward the river.

"Terry," I whispered. "I think there's a tapir on the beach." He was instantly awake. "What should we do?"

"Let's get him," Terry whispered back. "We've still got the gun." Tapirs were delicious and the Indians would be hungry when they got back. He picked up our .22 rifle and a box of shells.

Hugging the tree line, walking stealthily

from down wind, we closed in carefully. It was a big one, the size of a small cow with a long snout for a nose. Terry put the gun to his shoulder. Fired. The tapir winced and paused, looking around, confused. Another shot and he winced again, then started running toward the river for protection.

There was no point in being stealthy now. Terry and I both took off running, hoping to cut the tapir off before he reached the water. Surely he would fall soon from the wounds.

Leaping from rock to rock I got between him and the water, shouting and waving my hands, trying to turn him back. It didn't work. Either because of the pain or because he was so much bigger than me, he kept running, now directly at me. I turned and headed into the water myself, but in a split second he was even with me.

There was no time to think — I threw my arms around his neck and hung on for dear life as he charged deep into the river and went under before I could even get a good breath. Together we tumbled through a turbulent rapid, banging on submerged rocks. My lungs ached and I swallowed water, but I refused to let go. Surely Grandpa would be right downriver to help me. Ever since I was a tiny boy the Machiguengas had taken care of us. And then something caught my leg.

With the current pulling the tapir and me downriver and my leg caught on something, I was getting ripped apart, almost torn between two worlds.

My Dad saved me, pulling on my leg and telling me to wake up and get ready for school. *Oh yeah*, I remembered as my mind slowly switched from the dream to the reality. *School*. In the USA. A world away from my Machiguenga friends in Peru.

We were on furlough in Hartford, Connecticut. Having spent most of our early years in Peru's Amazon jungle, we weren't all that well traveled. If it hadn't been for furloughs every five years, we would never have gotten to see a foreign country like the USA.

Dad and Mom had been working in the Peruvian jungle for about 12 years with the Machiguenga Indians. As members of the Summer Institute of Linguistics and the Wycliffe Bible Translators, they had learned the language, devised an alphabet, printed a bunch of basic school books and translated a couple books of the Bible into Machiguenga. Now it was time for a change and a chance to visit friends and family and supporters in the USA.

There were about 350 people on my parents' mailing list. They were pretty much just names to us kids — about all we

knew of them was that 350 was a lot of
newsletters to fold, a lot of stamps to lick
and a lot of envelopes to seal every few
months. You could completely wear out a
tongue doing that, and believe me, Peru
didn't bother to make the glue on the
stamps tasty. Given our ages, Terry 12, me
11, Sandy 8 and Melody 5, you could figure
Terry and I had each licked about 4000
stamps apiece, and Sandy and Melody
about 40 apiece. Though they wouldn't
admit it, Sandy and Melody never had to
work as hard as we did.

The worst part of it was that those 350
friends were scattered around the USA. If
they'd all been in one city, we could have
just showed our pictures once, had fried
chicken once, mumbled "Yes, I know I've
really grown" once, answered "No, this
doesn't feel at all like home" once, said
"something in Machiguenga so the children
can hear what it sounds like" once and
returned to Peru on the next flight. We
wouldn't have had to do it all a hundred
times and sit scrunched into an old station
wagon without AC for two hundred and fifty
thousand miles in June, July and August in
the Mojave Desert.

On the other hand, we wouldn't have
gotten to see every tourist attraction
between Miami and Seattle and we
wouldn't ever have gotten to see McHale's

Navy and Gilligan's Island and Hogan's Heroes, so we'd have been pretty deprived culturally. To say nothing of getting to eat at Dairy Queen every week, which is where we stocked up on plastic banana split boats to take back to Peru with us. Those boats were perfect for making river boats using little motors and plastic parts that we salvaged from manufactured models that had more or less exploded on impact.

The real agony for us during our 1962 furlough, apart from just having to adjust to such a strange country, was that we were featured in a documentary movie made earlier that year in Peru. It was a pretty good overview of our organization's work in general and of my parents' work in particular. Back then people in church could actually sit still for a one-hour documentary, so we took advantage of their patience and showed it at every whistle stop we made between Miami, Los Angeles, Seattle and Maine.

"Where're y'all from?" some friendly gas station attendant would ask, and we'd show him our movie.

We had every line memorized and got so sick of seeing it that we'd resort to anything to get out of another viewing. Like the night we waited until the lights went out in the church and the movie had started.

"I'm going to take the three older kids

down to the basement to play hide-n-seek,"
Mom whispered to Dad. She never dreamed
that Dad would also sneak out with Melody
to go eat ice cream at Dairy Queen and leave
the movie projector unattended. We were
all back in our seats by offering time, of
course, thankful that the ancient projector
hadn't jammed.

We had a couple of wide-eyed night
monkeys to entertain us as we traveled.
Some people probably thought they were
better behaved than we were, but that's
only because they slept during the daytime.
At night they could get pretty unruly,
leaping from curtain rod to curtain rod and
hunting for food in our hosts' kitchens.
Anyway, after showing our marvelous but
by now monotonous movie to every church
in America and dressing up like Indians for
a thousand Sunday school classes, we
settled in Hartford so Dad could get his
master's degree in anthropology, which was
only slightly irregular because he had never
graduated from high school or college.

We arrived in Hartford just in time to
register everyone for school and moved into
an apartment on my parents' thirteenth
wedding anniversary. Since we didn't have
a stick of furniture, we threw foam pads on
the floor and celebrated by ordering a cake
from Mayron's bakery, just down the street.
Mayron's had made President Kennedy's

inauguration cake. "Wanna see the pictures?" the owner proudly asked us more than once.

I don't know if JFK liked his cake, but ours was pretty grand with strawberries and whipped cream all over it. That was back in the days when you could eat stuff like that without feeling like a heathen.

Bethel Baptist church had a special ministry to seminary students and one of their staff dropped in while we were eating our cake on the floor. The next day a whole truckload of furniture arrived out of nowhere, which of course meant we had to sit on chairs and eat off a table and sleep on beds from then on. Bummer.

We lived on the first floor of a three story apartment and the best thing about that apartment was the cheap rent, which was even cheaper by the time Dad had finished bargaining. Our Jewish landlord finally figured he'd met his match.

The other best thing about the apartment was the Pasha family that lived upstairs. They were staunch Catholics and we were staunch Protestants but we decided not to burn the place down over it and the Pashas became very special friends. I'm not sure if they thought of us as friends or mascots.

Since we lived on the first floor, we had the best access to the basement, which was dark and musty and creepy and full of useful trash. Terry and I salvaged some scrap lumber down there and a few wheels from the dump and made a little cart so we could haul our sisters around on it.

"I wish my kids could spend some time in the jungle learning to make stuff like that," Uncle Joe Pasha told Dad as he watched us play. "They wouldn't take so many things for granted." We wished we could afford to buy a wagon.

We were about as poor then as we've ever been, what with Dad and Mom both going to school and us having to eat Dunkin' Donuts every Saturday morning to make up for lost time and store up for the next five years. There were days when it was questionable whether or not we'd have food to eat the rest of the week.

One Sunday morning during a missions emphasis at church Dad talked to Jim Rose, a young engineer and his wife Phyllis about being missionaries. They attended a different church but had dropped in to see our movie and wanted to know more.

"Why don't you just join us for lunch," Dad offered. "Then we can talk as long as we like."

"Uhhh... is that going to be okay with your wife?" Phyllis asked. "She won't have planned on extra people for lunch and there might not be enough."

"God will provide," Dad answered confidently without asking Mom her opinion. Mom's opinion would have been that she should serve Dad for lunch.

No sooner had we all gotten home than Mrs. Pasha came down the squeaky stairs.

"I just fixed a big Sunday dinner but all of a sudden we've got to leave. Could you use it?" We said we'd think about it.

Phyllis ended up very supportive of Jim's desire to be a missionary — maybe she thought she'd never have to cook again.

Our junior high Sunday school teacher had already been a missionary and she had more guts than brains. Or maybe she wanted to prove that someone who had lived in Africa was just as tough as someone who had lived in Peru and certainly tougher than someone who had just lived in America. In any case, she accepted the challenge we threw at her.

"Next Saturday we'll all put on our roller skates and head out on the highway. The first person to quit loses," we dared. In the middle of a long steep hill twenty miles later, she finally gave in and called for a ride home. None of us could walk in church the next day. I still have a lot of respect for that saint, even if I can't remember her name.

One night Uncle Joe and Aunt Alice Pasha came down to our apartment for a visit. They weren't really relatives, of course, but we called them "aunt" and "uncle" just as we did the adults back in Peru. It was kind of an honor but they probably didn't know it. Anyway Uncle Joe said he was getting ready for hunting season and wanted to show us his new guns, a shiny pair of .22 rifles. We held them reverently, not wanting to leave a single fingerprint and I put one up to my shoulder to take aim at a lamp. Uncle Joe watched me closely, then asked why I was sighting with my left eye when I was holding the gun against my right shoulder. It was the first time anyone had figured out why I looked so weird shooting a gun and explained a lot about my marksmanship.

Uncle Joe went on and on about how fabulous these guns were and we were bubbling with envy when they got up to go.

"By the way," he said stopping at the door, "I really got them for you. For the jungle. Write and tell me what you shoot." And they left. My eyes blur, remembering.

Although Terry and I were a year apart in age, we had been in the same grade ever since Dad taught me second grade during a summer in the tribe. Now in Hartford we both went to an inner city junior high school that didn't have a clue what to do with boys like us. I mean boys that are interested in reading and writing and speak three languages and know something about the world, not that it was our fault. The school had some strange values. Like you could get in more trouble for stepping on the grass than for not studying.

In fact it happened to me one afternoon just as school got out. I was ecstatic to be free once more for the afternoon and in my abandonment took a shortcut between two sidewalks. A fellow student with a white vest and a whistle immediately shrilled at me and yelled for me to follow him. I couldn't have felt more humiliated in handcuffs.

Trembling, I followed my puny guard back to my homeroom on the second floor of the ancient junior high school. Unfortunately a tall, thin buzzard-looking lady was my home room teacher, which meant she would be the prosecuting attorney and executioner. Full of pride in himself and disdain for me, the whistle-blowing guard announced my terrible crime and raced back out to catch more hard-core criminals. The buzzard glared at me, wishing me to die on the spot so she could devour my quivering flesh and get on with her life.

"Did you really walk on the *grass*?" she hissed.

"Yes...well...uhh..." I would rather have faced a wild Machiguenga Indian with a blowgun.

"Where are you *from*!" she snarled,

making it sound a lot more like an insult than a question.

"Peru," I answered meekly. She hesitated slightly, apparently having never heard of it.

"And do they let you walk all over the grass in *Peru*?" she spat.

"Well... yes ma'am... we don't have sidewalks." I wasn't trying to be impudent, but didn't know what else to say.

"Well, we have them *here*," she reminded me in no uncertain terms, "and we expect you to *use* them. Don't *ever* let us catch you walking on the grass again." Somehow I escaped punishment, probably because she felt so sorry for me being from a place where there were no sidewalks. I felt sorry for people who could never walk barefoot across the grass.

In Peru we'd had teachers who were committed to teaching. Now we suffered through classes designed to bore. One math teacher in particular regularly screamed at us.

"You all are so stupid you're never going to amount to anything," she repeated over and over. I hope they've proven her wrong.

Terry and I had paper routes that year and about the only thing I remember about them is walking down dark musty halls in apartment buildings trying to collect our money. For some reason we lived through it, which was much more of a miracle than living through a dozen years with primitive Indians. Oh yeah, I also remember getting hit by a car once when I was throwing papers. The driver was terribly apologetic and wanted to take me to a hospital but I argued her out of it because after all I felt fine and I thought it was probably my fault. Now I realize that in America, where lawyers have a better feel for how serious an injury is than doctors do, I could've gotten more money from that little bump than I ever did throwing papers.

Hartford was also where I was baptized. It was a special step of acknowledging publicly what I believed privately, but to this day I wish I'd been baptized by a Machiguenga pastor in the Camisea River. It seems that would have been more appropriate.

At the end of our year in Hartford we paraded around the USA once again with our movie, which wasn't getting any better, then settled in Goshen, Indiana so Dad could study for one more year at Goshen College. This furlough business was turning into a life sentence.

The best things about Goshen was the big old house we got to live in for seventy dollars a month and the fact that Terry and I had to ride three miles to school on our bicycles in rain, sleet, snow and sun. If it hadn't been for that, I wouldn't be able to tell my boys how tough I had it compared to them. We did indeed slop through whatever the weather happened to be and many days ours were the only two bicycles in the rack at school. If only I'd thought to put goose grease in my hair and wear a coonskin cap my stories would be as good as Dad's.

Since Goshen was only nine miles from Dad and Mom's main supporting church in Elkhart, we went back and forth often. As we made some friends there, in fact, Terry and I made the round trip occasionally on bicycles, not realizing that in America teens aren't supposed to go more than one block without a car. A couple of families in particular made the trip worthwhile: the Beachams lived on a little creek that at least resembled something we were used to, so we spent hours at their house fishing, wading in the frigid stream, catching turtles and climbing their weeping willow tree. The Irelands lived out in the country and had twin daughters more or less our ages and Terry and I fell in love with them and although being in America was a dreadful thing for us, being in love at least put a little different spin on it and made eighteen miles on bicycles more tolerable.

Our junior high Sunday school teacher was Charles Miller and if you stick with these books long enough you'll find out that

God works in strange ways. Not that Mr. Miller was strange, except that he did... never mind... that's another story.

Our dog Chico came into our lives in Goshen, another of those things that you don't know whether to categorize as a blessing or a curse. His father was a terrier owned by a church deacon and his mother a Chihuahua owned by the church pastor and since they lived right next door to each other... well... there must have been a hole in the fence and the dogs never really grasped the ten commandments.

I can't say the terrier/Chihuahua cross was a particularly great combination, although he was at least a pretty brown color. Chico's mother was so little he had to be delivered by C-section even though he was small enough to fit into a teacup. From the start he was spoiled rotten and completely untrainable. We loved him dearly even if he never learned to sit, lie down, roll over or anything else useful. You'll never see a story about *him* in **Reader's Digest**. He yapped endlessly and Dad yelled at him endlessly and between the two of them the world was a much noisier place. At least Chico was small.

Chico managed to run out in the street one day and get hit by a car, sending Sandy into the house screaming that he'd been killed. In retrospect, that might have been good news. Dad, who would never have admitted to loving the yappy mutt, dodged through two lanes of traffic yelling his head off, salvaged Chico's bloody limp body and raced off to the vet, where we spent more money on Chico than we spent on me when I got hit by that car back in Hartford. We were learning to be more like Humane Society Americans every day — the Machiguengas would have just blown a little smoke into the wounds and hoped for the best. Chico survived, though he always had a bump over one eye and one ear that sort of flopped. He wasn't a particularly attractive dog anyway and people seldom noticed the flaws.

Goshen was where Dad called us all into the living room one awful night. "President Kennedy just made a pretty serious threat to Cuba," he said, "so I might have to go to war. We don't know yet what's going to happen, but I just want you to be prepared."

Since Dad had been in the Navy, he thought he might be called back into active duty. That prospect was frightening indeed — usually when Dad called us together to say he might die, it was because of amoebae attacks, which somehow seemed less threatening since we all had amoebas.

Then there was the horrible day in November when all of us students were called into a special assembly at school to be told that JFK had been assassinated. We got out of school early and peddled home as fast as we could.

"What are you doing home already?" Mom asked.

"President Kennedy was killed today," we said, "so they dismissed us." Mom laughed, not believing, then turned on the TV. The truth was there, stark and shocking. It was strange to think that our Machiguenga friends wouldn't know until we told them and then they wouldn't care.

Dad's thesis for his master's degree in anthropology was all about how the Machis figure out who's related to whom and if you think this book is boring, you should read his. Not that I ever have.

It's a little complicated but also pretty important, considering that all Machis considered themselves related to all other Machis in some way, but not in the same ways that we consider ourselves related to each other. Lots of considers in that sentence, but not as many as in Dad's book.

Can you imagine how complicated it gets having several thousand people all related to each other? I had one grandfather that was six years younger than I was and plenty of sons who were older. The nice part was that if we ever needed anything, we could just sidle up to a likely target and say, "Mother, would you...." Mothers always looked out for their kids, even if the kids were blonde beggars.

When you're translating the Bible into another language, you have to figure out what the relationships were among the Jewish people and then decide how to express those same relationships in, say, Machiguenga. That's not as straight-forward as it sounds. In Hebrew and English and Spanish, for example, Lot was Abraham's "nephew." In Machiguenga, since Lot was the son of Abraham's brother, he was Abraham's "son" too. So when Abraham said to God in Genesis 15:2-3, "You have given me no children...," it doesn't make sense to the Machis.

Well, Abraham and Lot got sorted out in a footnote at the bottom of the page along the lines of "Abraham was not the one who truly fathered Lot because Lot was fathered by Abraham's brother Haran and for that reason when it is translated in the white man's language it is said 'his nephew.' In Machiguenga it is said 'his son'."

Anyway, we were thrilled when Dad got his bachelor's degree one day and his master's degree the next day, even if we didn't think his book would make much money. We all dressed up and clapped enthusiastically because we didn't have to show our movie anymore. Finally, we could go back home to the world of our dreams.

For Dad and Mom, of course, it wasn't so simple. People who were strangers to us were precious family and friends to them — family and friends they wouldn't see for another six long years. As kids we cried when we left Peru and smiled when we left the USA. Our parents cried on both ends, their hearts buried in two places, their home straddling two continents, their closest family both village brown and suburban white.

# Chapter 2

*Epi and the Mad Bull*

Our return to Peru after furlough made the Lima newspaper, though not because of anything special we did. Actually, it was our dog Chico that attracted the attention.

Before we left the USA the Peruvian consul in Chicago said that Chico's vaccinations and health certificates had to be signed by a county clerk.

"I can't sign them," said the clerk. "We don't license vets. Try Public Health."

So we took the papers to Public Health, where the doctor swore that the vet was legitimate and then stamped the title of his office all over the papers.

In Miami we were informed that Chico had to have a special kennel for the plane. Though he was about the size of a huge rat, the airline wanted to charge us 20 dollars for a cage big enough to hold a donkey. Instead, we rushed downtown to Sears, bought something smaller for 12 dollars and raced back to the airport.

"You're going to have to buy a regular passage for the dog," a polite ticket agent said as we again tried to check in.

"A regular passage as in 179 dollars?" Dad asked incredulously.

"No, we just charge a flat rate plus so much per pound. How much does your dog weigh?" That ended up costing us another 12 dollars.

On the plane the stewardess came to tell us that Chico was lonely in the back. What that meant was that he was yipping nonstop and driving everyone insane. "Would you like him with you?" she asked. So he flew the rest of the way in our laps.

In Lima, customs was just waiting for a chance to enforce a new law about animals. They put Chico in dog quarantine to wait for a vet's checkup. Of course the vet never showed up, having bigger fish to fry, so Dad argued with the agents for an hour before he gave up and left Chico in custody, now waiting for someone to pay 48 dollars for his release.

In the meantime, photographers from *El*

*Comercio*, the leading newspaper in Lima had caught a whiff of what was going on, though we didn't know it until a picture of Terry and Chico showed up on the front page the next morning. Under the picture was a pretty sarcastic article ridiculing the government for charging a five-pound dog 48 dollars to get into the country. It didn't help and Dad finally paid the fee.

The next morning when we went to the airport to fly into the jungle, the airline said Chico had to fly as cargo. Another new ruling. It didn't matter that he had just flown from Miami to Lima in our laps, they said. We raced off to find the cargo office, where they weighed him and stuck him in the hold. Amazingly, he neither suffocated nor froze to death on the way, though I'm sure he let everyone within earshot know how he felt about being treated like a dog.

In the light of eternity, it probably won't be all that significant that we ended up having to pay 85 dollars to get Chico into Peru, but remember that we had already paid a fortune to the vet in Goshen after his car accident. By the pound, he was getting more expensive than caviar, and we couldn't even eat him.

Eventually we all arrived back in the wonderfully muggy heat of Yarinacocha, the jungle center for the Summer Institute of Linguistics. We only stayed enough days to unpack and repack, then flew two and a half hours south to the Machiguenga village of Camisea, where we had lived so often before going on furlough.

For the first week, while our house was getting cleaned out, all six of us lived in a little 14-foot by 16-foot hut with the rafters just four and a half feet off of the floor. The table and stove had to go outside the house until it rained, but in spite of the crowding it was a great chance to get reacquainted with our Machiguenga friends after two years away. Besides, by the time it rained the first time there was room for the table and stove inside because Terry and I were gone on an overnight hunting trip with our "Grandpa" Miguel. He was about 22 years old and was gracious enough to let us both help shoot the tapir we saw by the river in the morning. A dream come true.

The most memorable thing about our stay that summer was the cattle project. Dad had started flying calves out to different villages a couple years earlier so the Indians could develop a herd of alternative protein. The Machis didn't know a whole lot about cattle, of course and they didn't have fences to keep the cows from wandering wherever they wished eating clothes, school books, toilet paper and anything else that looked tasty.

The ominous black bull was supposed to

stay on the other side of the river but one night he waded across and scared a cow out of her wits. She ended up with a broken hip and we had to shoot her. Unfortunately, most of the Indians were still afraid to eat the meat, since they weren't familiar with it yet. That left just a few families to eat a whole cow, and no refrigeration. We salted big slabs and set up drying racks in the sun and over the fire to make jerky, but most of the meat ended up full of maggots. Shame we couldn't just eat them instead.

In the meantime, the bull, source of the problems in the first place, got pretty upset that the cow had died and kept coming across the river to sniff the blood where we had butchered her. He'd toss his huge head, stamp and paw with his hooves and bellow frightfully until someone had the nerve to chase him back across the river. That someone was almost always Dad, since the Machis weren't crazy about running around after mad bulls.

By this time, Dad and Mom had several colleagues helping them with the work — one Swiss couple from a mission near Pucallpa focused their efforts on working with the churches and another couple from our linguistic center worked on helping develop the bilingual schools. That meant that Dad and Mom could put more time into Scripture translation. Not that they were getting much done, what with people constantly interrupting them for medicine, fishhooks, cattle problems and general visiting. Besides, they couldn't find any good help in Camisea that summer, and without a good helper they were stuck.

No translator in his right mind would try to translate all by himself. The most crucial link in the translation process is a native speaker who can help make sure that what the Bible says in Hebrew or Greek is what it ends up saying in Machiguenga. Finding the right translation helpers is the key to everything, and not as easy as it sounds.

For one thing, Machiguenga Indians aren't used to sitting at a desk all day. Whenever they stop working they either eat or fall asleep, neither of which speeds the translation along. They don't think desk work is work.

For another thing, most Machis already have full lives. They have to clear, burn, plant and tend to their fields, make clothes, wash clothes, raise children, hunt, fish, recover from injuries and illnesses, build and repair houses and on and on.

Finally, most Machis don't have a clue how their language works or how to explain it to anyone else. To them, it's just something they speak and why couldn't anyone in the world speak it? Ask a Machi what the "na" particle means in the middle of a long verb and he'll say about the same thing you'd say if someone asked you why you call a chicken a chicken. "Huh?" you'd say.

In early September we all flew back to Yarinacocha so the four of us kids could get into school. Dad and Mom stayed with us for a couple of months and then we moved into the children's home so they could go back to work with the Machis.

Things had changed at the children's home while we were on furlough. The main difference was that Uncle Jim and Aunt Anita Price were now in charge of it, so we had to get used to a new set of "parents." Of course they weren't our aunt and uncle any more than they were our parents, but "aunt" and "uncle" seemed less formal than "Mr. and Mrs. Price."

Aunt Anita was easy to be with from the start – she was warm and loving and made fabulous cinnamon rolls and dill pickles, among other things. There were a lot of kids at the linguistic center who wished they could eat her cooking. She sewed costumes for school events and read stories to the younger kids and kept us all mostly scrubbed and dressed.

Uncle Jim was... well... Uncle Jim. He had a dry sense of humor and a mischievous bent and called Aunt Anita his "Sweet Roll." He would do anything for anybody who asked, but sort of came across like everyone who asked was a pain in the neck, so it took a lot of nerve to ask. As an adventurer and explorer he took us all on outings and trips, but never talked a lot unless the subject was boats or cameras or old cars. Terry, Sandy, Melody and I were scared to death of him for a while and the only reason we stuck around was that when he snapped at us, Aunt Anita would chuckle and reassure us that we weren't about to be eaten.

Uncle Jim's specialty at the children's home was pancakes on Saturday mornings. He just grabbed handfuls of this and that and ended up with huge power pancakes that would stick with you for the whole week, whether you wanted them to or not.

Uncle Jim and Aunt Anita became two of my closest friends but at the time we first met them, that would have been hard to predict.

With us happily back in school, Dad and Mom wanted to go back out to a Machi village and get on with the translation. They pondered and prayed about that a good bit, wondering where they would be most likely to get reliable help. Monte Carmelo seemed to be the answer.

One of the greatest boosts Dad and Mom had had in their translation work was the Pereira family, who lived in and around Monte Carmelo. In my last book I introduced Don Fidel – the brilliant half-Machi who would have graduated with highest marks from the University in Cuzco had he not been an Indian. When they wouldn't give him his degree, he returned to the Machi area to become a powerfully influential head man who had hundreds of Machis working for him. Mostly he was powerful and influential because he hired men to shoot people who disobeyed him. He produced a huge family, with the help of several wives.

Fortunately all of Don Fidel's children inherited his genius and he made sure that all of them learned Spanish fluently as they grew up. Though they didn't travel widely, they at least became familiar with the outside world and could go back and forth with ease. Of course some of them also inherited volatile tempers and moody personalities, which made it more or less easy to work with them depending on which mood they happened to be in.

For a while before furlough, young Dionisio Pereira had helped with the Scripture translation project. When Don Fidel first sent him to replace someone else, my folks weren't impressed. His first work wasn't all that great but Dad stuck with him for lack of anyone better. Not too much later Dio became a Christian and went to Bible school. He returned better prepared to help with the translation work and Dad and Mom discovered that he was extremely bright, growing in his own knowledge of the Scriptures and eager to see those Scriptures translated into Machiguenga. He had his struggles as a young single man and got inappropriately involved with a woman at one point, but Dad and he spent four months intensively working on I Corinthians and were ready to start on Acts when Dio drowned in a terrible boating accident.

"This has been the most difficult death we've ever had to deal with," Mom wrote in a letter to friends. "We've never been that close to someone who died and it was such a sudden shock. We have spent a lot of time with his brothers and sister, encouraging and comforting each other."

Don Fidel, with his white goatee and sparkling eyes, ruled the whole area around Monte Carmelo with an iron grip, but he had given Dad and Mom his permission to stay there. He said he had been studying all kinds of service and missionary groups and had decided that the linguistics group would be the most likely to do the Machiguengas some good. Meaning he was more interested in educational input than religious influences, but he would tolerate the latter in order to get the former. He had just recently told my folks that they could even begin to look for the scattered Machiguengas in the Kompiroshiato and Mantaro River valleys and establish schools there. On the other hand, he kept a very close watch on my parents and made sure that some of the people around Monte Carmelo never had contact with them.

By being in Monte Carmelo Dad and Mom hoped they could work with Epi, another of Don Fidel's sons. Epi lived about a 3-hour float downriver in Pangoa and had helped translate Mark and John several years before. Epi was brilliant, creative, a deep thinker and often a heavy drinker. When he was sober, he was the best. When he was drunk, he was awful. His personal spiritual journey would put a roller coaster to shame.

Although Terry, Sandy, Melody and I stayed at Yarinacocha, we had weekly 2-way radio contact with Dad and Mom so we could keep up on the news, and the news wasn't the best for a while. Epi was at his worst, having drifted into all kinds of trouble. He and his brother Alfredo fiercely opposed the Scripture translation work and did what they could to disrupt both it and the school where their sister Antonina taught 35 Machi children. At times he was a madman, standing outside her house in the night to shout threats and insults. On one particularly bad night he slapped Anto in the face so hard he knocked some of her bridgework loose.

At the end of November someone told Dad and Mom that Epi and Alfredo were coming upriver to Monte Carmelo for a visit. They stopped just around the bend from

Monte Carmelo to spend an hour drinking, so Epi was pretty well out of control by the time he arrived. He walked right past Dad and Mom's house to insult them and went directly to his father's house, where he and his buddies kept drinking.

About 3 a.m. Dad and Mom heard Epi coming down the path.

"I'd rather send my children to the devil than to this school," he shouted repeatedly into the darkness.

"To the devil," echoed his drunk brother in a voice that bounced off the bank across the river.

Dad went out on the porch to watch what was happening. In past rages, Epi had beaten up men and women and even killed men with his machete. Twice he had lain in wait, gun in hand, for planes from the linguistic center to arrive, saying he was going to shoot them down. Both times the water had been too turbulent for the planes to come. It wasn't a comfortable feeling, having him stomping and bellowing like a wild bull in the darkness, and this time Dad couldn't even just chase him back across the river.

Eventually Epi and Alfredo went down to the river on their own, got into their canoe and abruptly left, navigating the fierce rapids in the dark. In the morning one of the school kids filled Dad in on the gossip.

"Epi and Alfredo were drinking all night

and they got so mad they tried to get Maximo to join them but he wouldn't so they beat him up," said the eager tattle tale. "Then Don Fidel got angry and yelled at them that they were his two wicked sons and if that's the way they wanted to be then they couldn't stay in his house and he threw them out."

In the days ahead Epi repeatedly proclaimed that there was no God and he planned to serve only the devil. He promised to destroy every piece of translated Scripture that came his way and took his children out of school. A couple of years later he would do another about face, and in time he once again became a strong helper in the translation work. But for now, he had declared war as seriously as a Machi could, and no one could predict where that would lead.

In the meantime, Dad and Mom urgently wanted to keep translating. With Epi out of the picture, his brother Maximo was eager to help, so they plowed ahead, working through passages like the Christmas story, which was a lot harder than you might think, unless you think it's impossible, in which case it's just slightly easier.

It's a very special story, of course, about a God who loved the Machis, including Epi, so much that he actually sent a part of Himself to earth in the form of a man to provide a way for them to know Him personally. Now that was a novel concept!

As far as the Machis were concerned, God was the "Blowing One" in the sky who had given up on them.

Luke Chapter 2, so familiar to us, so foreign to the Machis.

"And it came to pass in those days," began the story, "that there went out a decree from Caesar Augustus."

Well now, that's a bit of a problem. The Machis had never had any system of government more complicated than a household headman who got his power either by being the dad of the family, or by being an exceptionally good storyteller who could out talk everyone else, or sometimes by being a particularly good shaman. There were a few men who had a lot of influence in larger areas, but they weren't exactly Caesar Augustus and they didn't send out decrees. Sometimes they got all their power by having workers with shotguns.

Anyway, the story goes on to say that whoever it was decreed that a census should be taken. The Machis didn't have a clue what a census was, though it would have been easy to take given the fact that they didn't count past four. "One, two, three, four, many." They had never cared how many of themselves there were, and hadn't a clue why anyone else would care.

Of course Caesar Augustus cared because he wanted all the world to be taxed.

Fine. But what's a tax? The Machis had never had money, and if they had they wouldn't have given it away to someone they didn't know. And besides, what did all that have to do with counting the number of people there were?

All that aside, this taxing was first made when Cyrenius was governor of Syria. As you already know, the Indians had never heard of a governor, or of Syria. Syria was just a place and we could make a map to show them where it was. Unfortunately most of them had never seen maps and hadn't a clue what they represented.

So everyone went to be taxed, each to his own town. What's a town? When Dad and Mom started their work, Timpia was about as large as a community got: one house for the Machis who lived there, one house for the Spanish landowner who made them work for him and eventually one house for our family. It wasn't exactly Bethlehem.

Anyway, Joseph went to the city of David. As you are already guessing, the city of David didn't mean nearly as much to jungle Indians with no sense of history as it did to the Jews, all of whom were in awe of the city of David and knew that from David's line there would come a Messiah.

Finally we get to some familiar territory. Mary was pregnant and about to deliver her baby. The Machis at least knew about women being pregnant, not that they would know about being engaged or betrothed.

Mary and Joseph headed for the inn where Mary gave birth to Jesus, wrapped him in swaddling clothes and laid him in a manger. Oh dear. What's an inn? What's a manger?

In the fields nearby, shepherds were keeping watch over their flocks, as you know. What you didn't know is that the Amazon Indians didn't keep animals except for dogs and the rare monkey, tapir or parrot that they caught alive. Those didn't exactly qualify as flocks of sheep. They had no notion of how or why you would have people sitting out in a field watching animals, as if you could see them anyway in the jungle. The Machis sometimes spent days looking for an animal to eat. Besides, what's a sheep?

By now, I suppose, this is getting a little tedious for you, but not as tedious as it was for my parents, I can assure you. No words for angels, no idea what the glory of the Lord was that shined around them, and on and on. That left a lot of holes in the story. I mean, it would lose quite a bit if you just said Mary was pregnant and had a baby.

With a lot of grinding, tedious persistence, Dad and Mom worked their way through each verse, looking for ways to say the unsayable. Caesar Augustus became the mighty one. A census became something where you went to be written into a book. The governor of Syria was the mighty one's henchman sent to watch over things in Syria. The inn was a house which was slept in from time to time. And so on, right through the sheep, which were given a name borrowed from Spanish, and the glory of the Lord, which in Machi says something like "they were lit up by God's light, like a lamp lights up those in a room at night."

Of course the Christmas story is only a small part of the Bible, and was only one small part of the whole translation project. Various helpers along the way worked for years to figure out how to help the Machis understand political systems, religious structures that included group worship, sacrifices, temples, religious offerings, prayers, educational systems that included teachers of the law, rabbis, pharisees, and on and on. They had no concept of a climate that got freezing cold, nor of a geographical area that had deserts, vineyards, donkeys, wells and seas.

To make matters worse, Machiguengas use verbs to express what we think of as abstract nouns, so things like mercy, grace, hope, love and faith all had to be converted into long, tangled verbs with an unbelievable number of prefixes and suffixes.

Believe it or not, the word for desert was one of the hardest to invent. Even after Epi traveled to the USA and went through the Mojave desert he couldn't figure out a way to describe it in Machi. Finally a man who had never seen a desert came up with a word that means "place where the atmosphere clears up as it arrives," or place where it doesn't rain. "That's right," agreed Maximo, "that would be a desert."

Eventually several Machis became good translation helpers and many got involved at one point or another. Irene, another Pereira sister, was Mom's special helper and was one of the most creative problem solvers in the translation work. She was the one who figured out how to say "dragon" in Revelation, using a certain kind of lizard as the root and adding descriptive affixes to make it bigger and fiercer.

In spite of the good help, it was a long time before the Gospels of Luke and Matthew were finally finished and printed. Four years later, Christmas morning, 1968, two remarkable things happened: the whole world listened as sophisticated astronauts read the Christmas story for the first time from lunar orbit and far below, out of sight in a tiny jungle clearing, a handful of barefoot, barely literate Machiguengas heard the Christmas story for the first time in their own language.

God heard it all: the astronauts reading in English from the moon and Dad reading in Machiguenga from Mantaro. Surely He had a big smile on His face.

# Chapter 3

## *The Airstrip*

"Kompiroshiato" probably isn't all that easy for you to pronounce, though it isn't even close to being the longest Machiguenga word there is. Machiguengas have a way of putting a whole lot of meaning into one word. Like "irapusatinkaatsempokitasanoigavetapaakemparorokarityo," which means something along the lines of "they will probably really fall head over heels into the water when they arrive but they won't stay that way, and this'll probably be the only time it happens." Little Machiguenga children can say words like that without taking a breath and they don't even act as if they've just done something precocious.

Anyway, to a Machiguenga, Kompiro-shiato means "palm leaf stream". To me it means "place where I almost starved to death and Mr. Claypool lost 46 pounds and we didn't get much done in five weeks." Which shows that I can get even more meaning into some words than they can. Anyway, I'll call it Kompi, pronounced "kombi," so you don't just skip this chapter.

By the mid 1960s there were quite a few educated Machiguenga school teachers and leaders living in established villages on the major rivers. For educational, medical and spiritual reasons, some of those leaders badly wanted to reach out to the rest of their tribe. It was no small ambition, given the Machis' tradition of living in small, isolated family groups in some of Peru's most inaccessible jungles.

Pedro Vicente and his petite, dimpled wife Adela were living in Monte Carmelo helping Antonina with the school when he decided to go find the Machis who lived in the Kompi River valley. They headed like pioneers for Kompi with their two little kids. Rafting, canoeing and mostly walking along barely visible trails, they eventually visited several dozen families living in tiny clearings on steep hillsides. Though I wasn't there, I can imagine how it went.

Pedro and Adela would walk into a clearing unannounced, Pedro ahead and Adela behind.

Anyone lucky enough to have an escape route would run into the jungle or hide, a survival instinct left over from the rubber hunting days when most outsiders came to kidnap and kill. In fact, these families lived where they did precisely because outsiders would have such a hard time finding them there. Anyone who got caught without an exit had the unwelcome job of welcoming the visitors. "Welcome" is a bit too enthusiastic of a word, of course. With frowning faces and desperate sideways glances, barely audible greetings would shuffle back and forth, starting with Pedro.

"Ainovi? Are you?"

"Ainona. I am. You've come?"

"I've come."

Having noted that everyone who was, was, and that everyone who had come, had come, there'd be some silent foot shuffling for a while.

"Sit."

"Heh eh," meaning "okay." They'd sit to continue their gripping conversation.

"Where did you come from?"

"Downriver."

"Is that right?"

"That's right."

"Where did you sleep last night."

"Downriver." Pedro's lips stuck out in the general direction.

"Is that right?"

"That's right."

While the small talk went on, everyone picked thorns out of their feet, shaved cracked calluses off with a machete or picked for lice, delicately biting each louse to be sure it was dead and then spitting it out. Any women or girls who hadn't escaped filled huge gourd bowls with fermented manioc drink, always kept in good supply for just such exciting occasions.

Pedro would of course get the first bowl — a couple of pints worth — and down it in one good guzzle, spilling dribbles out the sides of his mouth. Just to be polite, he'd have to finish all but the dregs, then toss them into the yard, wipe his chin and wait until it was his turn again. By the time it was over, he'd look three months pregnant and everyone would be talking a little more freely.

"We're building a village with a government school downriver."

"You're building a village with a school downriver?"

"That's right."

"Is that right. What's a school?"

What, for that matter, was a village or a government?

"If the government needs children for a

school," one Machiguenga asked, "why doesn't he have his own children." Many accused the teachers of wanting to collect the children together so they could be sold downriver.

It was always a tedious process introducing new ideas, and I grew up with oceans of admiration for the Machi men and women who risked their lives to sit in huts and guzzle gallons of hospitality while listening to their audience repeat everything they said, even if they didn't understand it.

Though some Machis were too afraid to move so close to anyone else, many did, and Kompi was slowly hacked out of the jungle. Pedro built a model home high off the beach's sandy ground, but most of the new arrivals just threw together tent-like shelters of cane and leaves. School children met on Pedro's front porch, writing on white rocks with bits of charcoal. When he first ran the Peruvian flag up the pole, one woman asked another, "What's he doing with that cloth, drying it out?"

For the first year, immigrants had to commute to their old fields for groceries, often taking days to go back and forth. When they weren't commuting, they worked to clear new fields, hacking down the jungle with new machetes and axes, burning off as much as they could after it had dried and then planting manioc, corn, papayas, bananas and sweet potatoes around leftover logs and stumps that would eventually be used for firewood. It was hard work and hard on the jungle, but all they knew to do. The school started without materials or supplies, the curriculum flowing out of Pedro's head.

Once Pedro got the community started, he needed some backup. He had promised the people a school and medical help but the closest place to get materials and medicines was a seven-day round trip by raft and canoe in the best of circumstances. He really needed an airstrip so small planes from the linguistic center could fly in with supplies and consultants. That's how I got involved.

"I'll go build the airstrip," I eagerly volunteered when I heard Dad talking about the need. I was thirteen and hadn't yet learned that if you're the only volunteer, you probably should've kept your mouth shut.

"Okay, if we can get someone to go with you." My dad was forty-seven and he'd learned a long time ago that if you were lucky enough to get one volunteer for jobs like this, you took him. Or maybe, as readers of my first book have suggested, he really didn't love me.

In the end we found one more volunteer, the lone survivor of a group that was pretty gung ho about helping with the airstrip until the details became more clear. Bill Claypool was a high school teacher who'd come to Yarinacocha for a couple of years. I'll call him "B.C." even though that makes him sound older than he was. It's better than "Mr. Claypool," which takes too long to read and makes him sound like some kind of swimming hole. Since I was his student I could never be so irreverent as to just call him "Bill."

"I'd love to spend a summer hiking and camping and working outside," said B.C. in a voice that was far more enthusiastic then than it was at the end of the summer. He was one of those multitalented men who'd done a lot of backpacking in the Sierras. "That'd be a perfect break from teaching." He probably should have said "break down."

Preparations for our trip included purchasing and then packing all of the tools and food we'd need for five weeks in the jungle. Mind you, the Machis got along quite well without Tang and oxtail soup mix, but we didn't think we could.

Since we didn't want to carry it all in over the trail, we carefully cushioned it for an air drop from a low flying airplane. B.C. had never pushed things out of airplanes before, but it wasn't hard to imagine what would happen to an uncushioned canned ham if it landed on a rock from 300 feet in the air going 80 miles an hour. Ham to Spam in one *wham*!

While we made our preparations, the rest of my family made theirs. They planned to spend the summer in Camisea, where Dad and Mom would continue their language analysis and community development projects and especially their Bible translation work.

As a special treat, some of my parents' friends in Indiana had sent their innocent and unsuspecting teenaged daughter Sharon down for a visit. She thought she wanted to see what our family's life was like, and especially wanted to spend some time in a Machi village. I'm sure she still has nightmares. Tim Townsend, whom we called "Towner," was one of our best friends from Yarinacocha and we invited him to join us in Camisea for a few weeks as well. One big happy family getting ready to fly unknowingly into a terrible Machiguenga tragedy.

We all flew together to Camisea in the potbellied Catalina flying boat. That was a wondrous and thunderous twin engine amphibious airplane from World War II with a pair of windows in back that looked like bulgy frog eyes. There were also little square windows in the tower that supported the overhead wing, and by worming and wriggling we could climb up into the tower and stick our arms out those windows, which was a pretty good thrill at 120 miles per hour, especially during rainstorms.

The first time the Catalina had landed on the Urubamba River, a thick crowd of wide-eyed Machiguengas and my mom stood watching from the rocks. Relative peace prevailed while the huge plane swam toward the beach, looking something like a fat version of the ugly duckling. But when the wheels went down, the engines revved to the max and the swimming monster suddenly roared and waddled out of the water in their direction, there was mass panic, with long-robed Indians falling over each other and tripping on the rocks as they fled for the jungle.

I'm sure the pilots, with their panoramic view up front, are still chuckling. Mom certainly is — the pell mell stampede got her laughing so hard she could hardly run. I think the Machis would all agree she could hardly run anyway, but that's hardly the point here.

This time the gathered Machis stayed for the whole show as we landed, pulled up on the beach and unloaded the Cat. We dumped fuel into 55 gallon barrels to store for future flights, carried off boxes of medicines and school supplies and food, and helped winch one of the Catalina's giant wheels out of a hole it had dropped into. The gnats on the beaches in July were ferocious — thick clouds of the tiny little buggers drove us to distraction or into the river. If we waded in until just our noses and eyes showed, like alligators, then all we had to swat and scratch was the top half of our heads. Or we could just stay completely underwater, though there was obviously a limit to that.

As soon as everything had been unloaded we all paddled and poled upriver to Camisea, where we'd spend the night. In high spirits we pulled up to the bank, and knew instantly that something was dreadfully wrong. There was no one to greet us. The only sounds were coughing and spitting. Virtually everyone in the village was incapacitated with measles and complications. A deathly pall hung over Camisea.

In a somber mood we hung mosquito nets and went to bed to sleep fitfully. By the time a pilot from the linguistics center came in the next morning with a Helio Courier float plane to take B.C. and me twenty minutes further up the Urubamba, we were eager to get out of Camisea.

We landed on the swift, clear water beside the village of Monte Carmelo and tied up just long enough to drop me and the rear door off in preparation for the air drop. Then "Woody," our pilot, took B.C. over to Kompi, where he made several passes as low as possible over the rocky beach by the new village.

"This is going to be a little tricky," Woody yelled at B.C. "We don't have a very large target and I've got to do some pretty sharp banking and diving. When I yell *'mark,'* shove the stuff out."

B.C., whose stomach couldn't bank and dive as fast as the plane, quickly turned as green as the jungle below. Every time Woody yelled "mark" he vomited a little more of his breakfast and shoved a few more bundles of cargo out the door as the bouncing plane swerved and pulled up for another pass. The Indians below must have wondered what in the world was raining on them and whether they really wanted us to come help them after all.

Not having had much practice as a bombardier, B.C.'s accuracy was less than stellar but he arrived back in Monte Carmelo confident that at least some of our stuff had hit the beach, and he was pretty sure nothing had flattened a Machi hut. Both his stomach and the plane were empty. Though we didn't know it at the time, the fun part was now over.

We spent the night in Antonina's house. Anto was one of my favorite people — a gorgeous school teacher with sparkly black eyes and a dry wit and most importantly a gold tooth that glittered when she flashed her stunning smile. I don't think she got along all that well with my folks or the other Machiguenga leaders, who thought she was arrogant, domineering and moody but I loved being around her. She fed us a great supper before sending us off to bed on her palm floor.

In the morning two guides showed up carrying their essential equipment for the trip: matches, coca leaves and a set of bow and arrows. Our essential equipment would have lasted them three lifetimes. We all hoisted our loads, said good-bye individually to everyone in sight and struck out for Kompi, ready to enjoy the out-of-doors.

Our enjoyment lasted about five minutes. That's how long it took to clear the edge of the village and start up the first mountain. Our guides had one speed – fast — whether they were going up or down. We had quite a number of speeds and none of them were fast. In ten minutes B.C. smelled like a draft horse and was blowing like a blue whale.

"Haven't they ever heard of switchbacks?" he wheezed to the heavens. "These aren't even trails." I didn't know quite what to say. Come to think of it, I hadn't ever seen a switchback in Machi country. It would be a terrible waste of time to go back and forth when you could go straight up.

The good news is that three days later, on the Fourth of July, we arrived in Kompi alive even if not so well. We'd been over three mountains up to 8,000 feet high, down a small river that we crisscrossed wading 128 times, down the edge of a steep slope to retrieve our little two-way radio that we'd dropped while trying to stay on a precipitous trail, more or less slept two nights in cane shelters, eaten honeycomb sheets of roasted beetle larvae and seen our barefoot guides once or twice each day. They probably wondered how anyone could walk so slowly without falling over. Or maybe their fear of the dead, which we smelled like, made them keep their distance.

"All I've got to say," B.C. said for both of us, "is I'm sure glad we're going to fly back out of here. That's got to be the toughest hike I've ever been on. It only took three minutes in the plane!" I don't think he cared any more about getting a good break from teaching school, but now he was trapped.

After all our effort, no one seemed particularly excited that we'd made it. No one, in fact, said a word. From a distance several of them just sat and watched us gasp for air, like fish lying on the sand. Fortunately, before the silence became too awkward, Pedro splashed across the river to greet us warmly, first shaking B.C.'s hand and then mine. That broke the ice. Adela and her little slave girl came next, then a bystander in a tattered robe. Once he had learned the handshake, he showed a wrinkled old man just how to do it.

The old man, mastering handshakes in two tries, taught every other man and boy in the village, making sure they did it just right. Each one started with B.C. and then moved on to me. We appropriately asked each and every one if he "was," and he said he "was" and "had we come?" and we said we had come. Once we were sure everyone was and everyone was sure we had come, the greetings were once again over.

Adela brought us some roasted manioc, a starchy root that Machis consider a gift from the heavens. She also offered to wash our clothes, which we considered a gift from the heavens. We bathed in the cold river, ate the warm manioc and considered ourselves home.

During the next couple of days we set up housekeeping in a new shelter with a double bed built of cane poles about two feet off the ground. It wouldn't really have taken two days just to organize our stuff, of course, especially given the fact that about half of our air-dropped supplies had either smashed on the rocks or gone into the river. Still, we worked rather slowly, since B.C. had a badly swollen ankle and my feet were covered with blisters from wearing boots over the trail. We read books and tried to fix our .22 caliber survival rifle and set up the radio to report that we'd made it.

The radio didn't work. Its plunge down the mountainside had apparently knocked loose some of its bowels and we faced the prospect of five weeks far from help with no contact to the outside world. B.C. was desperate to talk to his wife so he dried the radio's guts out really well, scraped and tightened random bits and pieces with his pocket knife and tried again. He was no electronics whiz but this time the receiver crackled and squawked and we heard the radio operator at Yarinacocha loud and clear. Since the transmitter still didn't work, there was no way to let everyone know that we'd made it to Kompi, that over half of our food hadn't made it, that B.C. still loved Mrs. C. and that he already missed her cooking.

Fortunately I faithfully kept a journal, which leaves me several options for telling the rest of this story. I could just do a page-by-page transcription, which would bore you to tears and would therefore most accurately reflect how the summer went. Or I could eliminate all of the poor and repetitive writing in the journal, which wouldn't leave much of interest, would make the story too short and would give away the end of the story too quickly. Not that you haven't already guessed, considering that I've already said our only consolation after the walk in was that we'd be able to fly back out.

I'll set the journal to one side, hold it in

reserve to prove to B.C. that what I'm about to say really happened and just recount the highlights, which were stretched pretty thin. So were we by the time it was over.

First there was the work. Like cutting down the jungle with machetes and axes. It's hard to imagine how many huge trees and bushes there are in a space 20 yards wide by 280 yards long, which was the size of our subregulation airstrip. It wasn't subregulation because we were lazy, but because there really wasn't any level ground 300 yards long, and we weren't about to move the mountain at the end of the strip, with or without faith the size of a mustard seed.

Apart from the strip itself we would have to clear a substantial approach, since the pilots didn't think they could roar around the blind bend in the river, buzz the tops of 100 foot trees, dive vertically toward the end of the airstrip, level off at the last nanosecond, stick the plane to the runway, jam on the brakes and skid to a stop before hitting the mountain. They just don't make pilots like they used to. The point is, we had to clear an approach, so that although they'd still have to do most of the above, they wouldn't have to dive over the edge of the 100-foot trees.

In between working on clearing their new fields and building houses the Machis, under Pedro's guidance, had already cut down quite a lot of the jungle where the airstrip would be. That left mostly the approach, which they hadn't thought about. We lost a lot of skin on our hands while working on that approach.

Sometimes it was a half day's work to cut down one tree, especially if it was four feet across and had huge buttress roots that looked like reinforcing walls holding up the tree. Usually someone would have to build a shaky scaffolding out of poles and vines so they could do the initial cutting ten or twelve feet off the ground, where the buttress roots weren't so big. That made for a precarious perch, but the Machis could cut away with hairline precision.

When I tried it, I considered myself lucky if I hit the tree at all without getting knocked off the scaffolding by the impact. The Machis didn't let me do much cutting up there, since they wanted their airstrip before the end of the Millennium and didn't want to take time out to bury me.

The awesome Goliath trees never fell easily, and never fell alone. The Machiguengas are old hands at clearing jungle, so we would prepare for a giant's fall by notching every smaller tree in its path, chopping perhaps a third of the way through each trunk. As we worked, we'd listen hour after hour to the thunk, thunk, thunk of the ax hacking chips from the kingpin, and when it started to crack, jiggle or sway we'd run for our lives, leaping over logs and slaloming around tangled bushes.

It's impossible to describe the thunderous, crashing roar when one of the Amazon's finest trees toppled, its massive trunk and enormous branches knocking over everything in its path and setting up a chain reaction that eventually knocked down everything we'd notched and then some. Winds from millions of rushing leaves blew in our faces. The ground shook as tree after tree smashed on the forest floor. As dominoes go, this was life on a pretty grand scale.

"Ario," a Machi would say in the hushed aftermath.

"That's that," someone would repeat. And that was that.

Once the trees and undergrowth had been cut down it had to be burned, since not even a madman would try to haul off the tons of tangled mess by hand. Until everything dried out there wasn't much to do. Fortunately July and August are in the "dry season," a relative term of course, and therefore great months for burning off airstrips. Unfortunately that July and August were exceptionally rainy. Our flawless plan had been to flatten, inflame, fill and fly away finished. Instead, we fumed in frustration.

If you were reading my journal instead of my highlights, in fact, you would be in despair. You probably are anyway. Day after day we'd optimistically say to each other, "It looks like we can burn tomorrow," only to be wakened by a drenching rain during the night. Sometimes there would be clear skies for a couple of days, so that our soggy spirits dried out with the brush. Then, as we struck the first match, the heavens would open, drowning the match and our hopes.

Sometimes thunder and lightning rocked us. Other times soft drizzles gently soaked the jungle for hours on end. It could rain out of a clear sky, whether or not there was a ring around the moon. Red sky at night and red sky in the morning both ended up wet. We got pretty adept at predicting the weather: if we wanted to start a fire the next day, it would either rain that night or start pouring as we waded across the river with our matches. We could even make it rain by talking about matches. Or just thinking about them.

The days crawled past at a snail's pace. For hours on end we mostly sat in our hut reading, carving wooden trinkets that even my mother wouldn't like, making ax handles, telling stories, and listening to the drip, drip, drip of rain drops off the eaves' leaves. To relieve the boredom during brief periods of sunshine, we sometimes went for walks, not that there was anywhere in particular to walk to, or went swimming, though the river was cold and shallow and often muddy from the rains. Once the rifle was fixed, we went hunting for wild turkeys and other game, usually unsuccessfully.

On one particularly long afternoon I dragged a balsa log into the water, wrapped myself around it and shot off downriver, evidently hoping to end my life in exhilaration rather than depression. B.C. and the Indians thought me crazy, but at least I had a story at the end of the day. And a pretty banged up knee—the rapids were a little wilder than I'd planned. Although he laughed at me, within a couple of weeks Pedro had tried it too. He was probably going a little bonkers himself.

The good news is that sometime during the first couple of weeks, for no reason in particular, our radio transmitter started working intermittently. Not that we received good news. From the sound of it our airstrip problems were minor compared to life in Camisea, where the measles epidemic was going full force, and my whole family was battling for our friends' lives.

All in all, neither Camisea nor Kompi were turning out anything like we'd planned, and none of us were particularly upbeat as we shouted back and forth through the static on our radios.

# Chapter 4

## *The Measles*

The measles had invaded Machiguenga territory quietly. A river trader with a sick Indian in his boat stopped at each village to buy and sell and dropped off a few germs here and there. Since they hadn't yet been immunized, the Machis soon began to drop like fall's leaves. Those who could still run disappeared into the jungle, spreading germs to each little household along the way. During the height of the epidemic, 149 of the 150 Machiguengas who lived in Camisea were so sick they couldn't walk.

The only healthy person in the village

was Doro the school teacher, who'd had the measles years before. Until my family got there, she was the only one who carried water, kept fires burning, spoon fed the worst off and doled out the limited medicines she happened to have. A brown Florence Nightingale, exhausted and desperate.

Dad and Mom and each kid had their own set of patients — even eight-year-old Melody went from hut to hut with a pot and a spoon. Scrawny, dehydrated Indians lay in their houses too weak to crawl outside to the bathroom. Bronchitis, ear infections, pneumonia and dysentery took advantage of sickly bodies and hopeless spirits. One man, trying desperately to get some fish, threw his line and hooked his own eye, blinding himself. Life boiled down to teaspoons of water or soup every fifteen minutes day and night for emaciated adults and their skeletal children, plus sponge baths, eardrops, aspirins and antibiotics. Sometimes the only way to help was to sit with the dying to lend moral support to the living.

When the supply of medicines ran dangerously low, Dad consulted Dr. Eichenberger by radio.

"We've got a lot of people with racking coughs. What do we do for them?"

"Do you have...."

"No, we're out of that."

"Do you have..."

"We've run out of that too."

"Well, do you have sugar and kerosene?" After several more attempts, Doc was groping for basics now.

"Yes..."

"Okay. Take a spoonful of sugar and mix in a couple drops of kerosene. That'll be better than nothing. Just don't tell the Indians what's in it."

Dad mixed a trial batch and spooned some into one patient's mouth.

"Kerosene," whispered the Indian with a grimace. As if he wouldn't know.

Many times the medicines and liquids and the kerosene weren't enough. Then inevitably, came trips to the sandy beaches to bury the dead. B.C. and I, still in Kompi working on the airstrip, heard the sad stories over our little radio.

Monikashio, or "Monkey" to us, was unusually close to his young wife Margarita and their infant son. Gaunt and feverish himself, he still tenderly cared for them and his despair deepened as he helplessly sat watching them waste away. Eventually Margarita's milk dried up and the tiny boy, a delicate skeleton wrapped in parchment, died.

Mom had just gotten back from helping bury the baby when messengers came to get her.

"Margarita is dying too," they said. "Can you come?" "Can you come?" A desperate plea repeated often through the years — a last hope that the outsiders would be able to do something, anything at all to save a mother or father, son or daughter.

Margarita was indeed slipping away. Maybe she just gave up when her baby died. She lay on a dirty mat, her dull black eyes huge in a skull that had been shaved to keep spirits from grabbing her hair. Unswallowed water dribbled out the side of her mouth. Her body, filthy and half naked, showed every bone. Her breath rattled in her throat.

Mom joined Monkey and his sister on the floor beside Margarita. A flickering homemade kerosene lamp threw moving streaks of light on the dark walls. Mom listened as the other two talked quietly, and became so completely absorbed in their conversation that she didn't even notice when Margarita stopped breathing.

"She's quiet," Monkey said, his eyes wide and fear lacing his voice. He snatched an old gourd off the floor and with all his remaining strength smashed it against Margarita's forehead. Mom winced and waited for Margarita to scream, "Stop! Stop! You're hurting me. Why are you doing this?" Instead, the only voice was Monkey's.

"Now you see how angry we are with you!" he hissed. "Now you'll go away and leave us alone. Now you won't take us with you. We *hate* you. We've never wanted you here." Alive, she was his precious wife. Dead, his dreadful enemy. The sooner they could get her away from the house, the better, but the trip downriver to bury her would have to wait for daybreak. It would be a night of fear, wondering who else her spirit would grab to take with her. Those with long hair cut it off to at least get rid of one handhold.

Agosto was one of the boys Terry and Towner helped treat. He was sixteen, just two years older than they were. When Agosto died, no one in his family was strong enough to bury him and no one else would come close so Terry, Towner and Sandy got the job.

In the morning Terry hoisted the mat-wrapped body over his shoulder and carried him to a canoe.

"What are we supposed to do with him?" Terry asked Dad.

"The main thing is, lay him with his face up and his head pointed downriver," Dad explained. "His family will want to be sure his spirit can get to the river and head downstream as fast as possible so it won't come back and drag them off."

The burial ground was a sandy area in the jungle by the river, forty-five minutes down from Camisea. Nerves taut, Terry and Towner quietly pulled the canoe up on the sandy bank. Dozens of buzzards startled into the air, their wings swooshing and flapping. The sinister black birds, looking like grim undertakers, landed close by on surrounding branches, staring down their hooked beaks and impatiently waiting for a chance to eat some more of the corpses that hadn't been buried deeply enough.

"Look at those tracks," Terry whispered. The jaguar's feet were as big as Terry's hand and frighteningly fresh. Remains of Machis lay exposed on the ground, decomposing and partially eaten. Terry loaded his .22 rifle and gave it to Sandy so she could stand guard while he and Tim dug the grave.

"How deep are you gonna go?" Sandy asked. Her voice trembled and her hands shook.

"Well, they always say 'six feet under'," Terry answered, starting to dig. "So I guess that's what we'll do. If we don't go deep enough the animals will just dig him up and we'll have to bury him again."

The sandy soil came out quickly, and soon Tim and Terry were in a hole five and a half feet deep. Without warning, there was a loud crash. Terry vaulted out, heart hammering, grabbed the gun and aimed it right at... a tree limb that had broken off.

"Let's get out of here," Towner urged. They picked up Antonio's body, dropped it into the hole face up, flung the sand in on top of him and hurried back to the canoe.

"I remember," Mom recalls, "that when they got back home they waded into the river and washed and washed and washed as if they could just scrub hard enough to get rid of the memory."

Late on another afternoon, Mom and Sandy went to visit Teresa, who was precariously sick but at least still alive.

"Why is she just laying out in the sun?" Sandy wondered, eyes wide. "They didn't even put her on a mat." Teresa had just been dumped, a barely breathing, pathetic heap of skin and bones.

"They're afraid to have her die inside the house after dark," Mom whispered. "They think she'll take them with her."

No sooner had Mom answered than Teresa's husband and brother rushed out with a mat, wrapped her in it, tied the ends shut and rolled her down the bank to their canoe. They paddled off and later returned just as the sun set, still looking over their shoulders. No one said whether or not she was dead when they piled the sand on her.

Melody was the only one in our family who hadn't had measles. She came down with a rip-roaring case.

"*Promise* me you won't bury me in the sand," she cried. "I want to be buried at Yarinacocha so the animals won't eat me."

Night after long night Mom read her books, trying to take her mind off the dreadfully sick Indians around her.

In the midst of all the pain, there were a few victories. One eleven-year-old boy hadn't pee'd for so long his bladder locked up and he couldn't release it. His whole belly swelled until he looked pregnant, but without catheters there was no way to help him.

"I'm going to give him some belladonna," Dad finally decided.

"What good will that do?" Mom asked. She was always a bit skeptical of his brews, and almost never let him experiment on her.

"I don't know, but it can't hurt. He's about gone anyway." Belladonna was a drug that Dad used to cure everything from upset stomachs to sleeplessness. I think it was really an antispasmodic designed to relax intestines during battles with dysentery, but he was never much inclined to read directions and limitations. If it would work on one thing, it would surely work on another. I think he learned that from the Indians, who never had much variety to choose from.

Anyway, to everyone's surprise but Dad's, the belladonna worked a miracle. The boy relaxed and they stood him outside his hut, naked, where he went for the world record. Anyone healthy enough to attend the spectacle laughed and joked and cheered like they were watching a home run. And run. And run. And run.

Altogether, fifteen Machiguengas died that summer just in Camisea. The measles epidemic spread to other villages, to other tribes, to the most tangled corners of the jungle. In places where there was no medicine, where there was no one to help, death came rattling far more often.

Back in Kompi, B.C.'s and my food supplies were getting finished off and our airstrip wasn't. By the time B.C. and I had been in Kompi for three weeks, we knew we were in trouble: food was becoming a major issue for us.

It wasn't that there wasn't any food. In fact, I faithfully described in my journal what we ate for every breakfast, lunch and supper, as if I somehow thought it would be fascinating to look back on. It isn't, of course, since it was all the same. Same, same, same.

The Machis took good care of us, but had little variety to offer since their new fields hadn't begun to produce yet. By walking a couple of hours downriver they could harvest manioc, sweet potatoes and some roots a little like white potatoes, but that was about it. That's sort of like a diet of white bread, rice and potatoes, except that white bread is probably better for you.

Pedro had a shotgun and used it on regular hunting trips, though big game was scarce in that area. He sometimes came back with wild turkeys or other large birds and Adela always came over with a more than generous portion for us. The rest they shared all around the village, trying to keep people happily fed so they wouldn't just go back to their old homes, which is pretty much what we wanted to do.

B.C. and I could have been more helpful with the hunting if we'd had anything but our .22 survival rifle. It was a clever, lightweight gun whose barrel unscrewed and slid into the plastic stock, making it conveniently compact to carry. Unfortunately, as I said in the last chapter, it didn't work at all when we first arrived in Kompi. I suspect B.C. was swinging it at branches and using it for a walking stick. In any case, he eventually got it fixed to the point that it would actually fire a bullet, which was a bit of an improvement.

The problem was that we never knew where the bullet would go. In fact, the gun was so unpredictable that in a survival situation, I'd have used it for a club, since all the bullets did was scare away precious game. We spent many fine hours shooting leaves and twigs and anything else that happened to be within twenty feet of what we were aiming at.

Anyway, we ate lots of manioc and sweet potatoes and sorta-potatoes. I had a bit of an advantage because I'd grown up eating manioc and thinking it was wonderful stuff. B.C. hadn't grown up with it and "wonderful" wasn't even close to being one of the words he'd have used to describe it. He'd have said something like "too dry to swallow without a gallon of water to flush it down."

We had manioc smoked, roasted, boiled, french fried and mashed and after enough days of that, it all started tasting like wallpaper paste no matter how it was fixed. In fact, turning traitor to my great upbringing, even I quit thinking it was wonderful.

Once in a while we got a reprieve. Like the afternoon a neighbor surprised us with a big basket of bright orange oranges that he'd found growing wild in the jungle. This particular man hadn't ever shown much interest in us before. He was tall and skinny and had hair that went every which way, kind of like Einstein's but black. His face was always smudged bright red, his teeth were black from chewing coca leaves, he had a withered leg that gave him a pronounced limp and his eyes had a pretty wild look in them. Even so, to us he looked like an angel when he handed us the oranges. Though the Machis have no way to say "thank you," we said "good ... good ... good" nine or ten times to make sure he knew we were grateful.

With all of the slobbery anticipation of a royal feast I peeled the first orange, ready to ward off the scurvy that we were sure was already weakening the capillaries and blood vessels in our gums. By the time I took my first big bite, our new friend wasn't anywhere in sight, which turned out to be for the best. My lips froze solid, my fillings shot electrical charges all over my head, involuntary chills raced around my body and my skin turned into an Andean range of goosebumps. That orange, by a wide margin, was the sourest citrus I'd ever sucked.

"How is it?" B.C. asked. He hadn't been watching closely.

"It's great!" I said. "Try a bite." He did. I wish I'd had my camera ready.

Well, I figured that whatever scurvy did it wasn't as bad as what those oranges would do, so I never ate another one. B.C., on the other hand, was more disciplined and he wanted to live long enough to see his kids again. After several tries, he just threw away the inside and ate the peelings, which weren't quite as sour. We even made some orangeade by squeezing sugar cane and adding orange juice to it. One drop of orange juice in a tall glass of sweet water was about as strong as I could take it. All I can say is those oranges lasted a long long time, and we weren't terribly enthusiastic when our generous friend limped in with a huge smile and a dozen more a couple weeks later. I don't think we said "good" even once. It didn't take a genius to figure out that the reason we got so many was that the Machis couldn't stand them.

Our biggest culinary break came one afternoon when I was downriver with the Indians helping dig manioc and potatoes. It was an all-day affair, but the long walk and hard work were a nice change from sitting around watching the rain clouds grumble and cry.

When we got back home late in the afternoon, my heart jumped and my salivary glands lept to attention: there were pineapple peelings scattered in front of our hut. Oh joy oh delight oh glory and thank you God and thank you B.C. for having it already peeled and ready. I ducked my head under the eaves.

"Did someone bring us a pineapple?" I asked with bouncing enthusiasm.

"Uh huh," B.C. answered with a guilty shadow drifting across his face.

"Where is it?"

"I... uhhh... ate it," he said without looking at me.

"All of it?" I was looking for a weapon.

"Uh huh."

I wanted to bang him in the belly with our useless gun until the pineapple all came back up, but I didn't. Instead I crawled around and kind of gnawed at what little morsels had come off with the peelings, just like a roach would raid the crumbs under your sink. From what I could tell, it had been a pretty good pineapple.

As I said, we weren't going to starve, but by the time B.C. described our situation to Mrs. C. over the radio a couple of times, she thought he would be dead within days. Frantic, she begged the aviation coordinator at our linguistic center to send a plane out with more supplies.

"It would be too expensive," he said. "Besides, everything would probably just land in the river again."

"My husband's dying and he doesn't have life insurance and I'll be left alone with two little children," she cried.

"He'll be all right," he said.

"You don't know him," she pleaded. "He passes out if he misses coffee break." It was all to no avail. No sympathy from me, either. At least he got a pineapple.

On July 30, a full month after we walked in, we were in the doldrums. For breakfast a man had brought us two more sticks of roasted manioc. Shortly after he left, Adela brought us another two. Then the village headman's daughter showed up with another huge piece, and we already had two pieces leftover from the night before. Our whole G.I. tracts were already plugged with paste just waiting for a flush.

We sat chewing our cuds for a long time, planning.

"We aren't gonna get it done." B.C. made it sound like an execution.

"I don't think so," I answered, which was pretty obvious since there were still trees all over it and airplanes can't land on stumps.

"So we're gonna have to walk out." The method of execution, like hanging or lethal injection. He sounded like either of those would be preferable, and his face looked about as happy as it did right after he took his first bite of orange.

We discussed the logistics and the options, and since there weren't much of either one we mostly chewed and tried to swallow.

Just before noon I vaguely heard Pedro talking to two of the other men.

"I'm going across to see if it's dry enough to burn."

"You're going across?"

"I'm going across." Since I was feeling cross, the repetition bugged me.

"Okay then, you go across."

We'd heard it so many times before I didn't even tag along.

"I'm gonna go sit outside for a while," B.C. finally said. I started to join him when he suddenly jumped up and pointed across the river, where flames shot fifty feet in the air and sent up enough smoke to darken the sun. In ecstasy we raced across the river to take pictures and watch, and to listen to the loud popping when sections of bamboo exploded. Like a starved monster the fire devoured hundreds of trees in a matter of hours, leaving charred skeletons and blackened earth.

"Cool," said B.C., though it was anything but. "Now we can finally go to work." Of course we only had a few days left, but at least we'd finish strong.

The next morning for the first time we could actually see where the airstrip should be. Which wasn't quite where we'd burned, of course. We marked some new boundary lines, showed Pedro what needed to be done, and began to clear.

In the end, we didn't get very far. Between rain showers, we set more fires and hauled off charred logs. We started smoothing out small sections, scraping humps into burlap bags and dragging the dirt over to holes and hollows. It was slow, backbreaking work, and our three days of effort barely un-made a dent, so to speak.

Preparing for our departure, we gave away most of what we owned to the Machis, which I've heard is one warning sign of a planned suicide, and went for short conditioning hikes, though I suppose it was a little late for that.

At 2:00 p.m. on August 5 we set off for home with two little bags of essentials and six packages of oxtail soup that we'd been saving. It was really too late in the day to be starting out, considering that it would take several hours to get over the first mountain. Still, we couldn't stand to wait one more day.

By the time we'd crested the mountain and headed back down the sun had set. In blinding darkness that mocked our flashlights we fumbled along behind our guides, stumbling over roots and grabbing onto anything within reach, including thorn trees, to stabilize ourselves. The Machis were afraid to stop in the jungle, so on we trudged, fortunately crashing and banging loudly enough to scare whatever wild animals there might have been in our path. The wildest animal in my path, of course, was B.C., but I usually avoided tripping over him even when he fell.

When we finally got to a small river we tumbled to the ground, forced down some boiled manioc and slept where we lay. Not that we actually slept, you understand, but at least we were there until morning.

After a cup of soup and water we started off again in the early dawn, feeling damp and ragged. B.C. looked a bit like a flimsy wire coat hanger that's about to bend and drop its clothes. We slowly worked our way up the Shimaa River, crossing back and forth through the shallow water, pausing just long enough at noon to roast some manioc and boil some green bananas, which are pretty good for roughage but taste a lot like particle board. Termites would love them.

That night started off okay, what with our very satisfying supper of oxtail broth, roasted manioc and toasted caterpillars, which are better than they sound but only if you're starving. We went to sleep under makeshift cane shelters, lying on the cold ground and drifting off into fits of shivering sleep. For what seemed to be hours I forced myself not to look at my watch and then, sure that the sun would be up soon, I glanced. 7:30 p.m.

At 10:00 the leaf cutter ants found us. Leaf cutters are big red ants with huge pincers on their heads and they make narrow trails up to three miles long as they march through the jungle searching for just the right leaves to take back to their underground nests. Actually, they use the leaves sort of like compost — as the leaves rot a fungus grows on them, and the ants eat the fungus. They must have thought they'd stumbled on a fast food joint when they discovered our camp — everything we owned already had fungus on it.

Not even the Machis, who live with these inconveniences all the time, had any suggestions for fighting off the ants. We basically sat and waited while they meticulously cut up our clothes, shoelaces, journals and camp gear into puzzle shaped pieces, then trooped off following their weird instincts. It wasn't as fun as it sounds, since we couldn't see them and whenever we irritated them they'd make a point of stabbing their pincers into us. "The ants go marching two thousand by two thousand..."

The ants left just as a cold rain started, soaking everything they had left behind. I waited for what had to be several hours before finally succumbing to the temptation to check my watch again. 11:00 p.m.

In the morning, which finally came after about a hundred hours of darkness, I saw a chicken-sized bird perched on a log near our shelter. In my taxonomy of the universe there are two kinds of animals: edible and non-edible. The hungrier you get, the bigger the edible group gets, so I asked one of our guides for his bow and arrows. Though he was skeptical, having seen how useless we were with a gun, he handed me his weapons and put his hand over his mouth so I couldn't see him laughing.

The bird stayed put in spite of my clattering approach. Perhaps it was as cold as I was, or maybe it just hadn't ever seen a white man who could use a bow and arrow. Whatever, I carefully drew back on the bowstring, released the arrow and by some great act of God, I drilled the bird right through the heart, shocking everyone including me. There wasn't much left by the time I'd plucked and gutted it but at least I got the reputation of being a mighty hunter. I've never been able to hit anything smaller than a barn since, lending credibility to the notion that this was a special provision.

We finally left the Shimaa River, again crossing it over 120 times, and slogged up our highest mountain in a pouring rain. All day cold wet leaves slapped us, the trail turned to mud, our blankets got soaked and our shoes filled with water. Finally, in an early gray darkness, shivering, teeth chattering, blue inside and out we each had a couple bites of my roasted bird and then once again lay down on the cold ground. It would be our last night out, we hoped.

Three hours into our walk the next morning we startled an agouti, which is sort of like a twenty pound version of a cross between a tailless chipmunk and a rat.

They taste great and when this one jumped into the stream in front of us, B.C. came back to life before my very eyes. Our guides were way ahead of us, which they always were since they couldn't walk as slow as we could, so we were on our own without weapons. In that instant I saw the raw survival instinct of our caveman ancestors fill B.C.'s broken body. We flung our packs aside and both grabbed rocks as we raced after the agouti, which had obviously eaten better than we had in the past few weeks.

"Quick, get him headed back," I shouted as I raced downstream after him, heaving rocks to get his attention. The stream was swift, but shallow and rocky. Gasping for breath, I tripped and slipped and fell and dove and finally got the agouti to head back upstream where B.C. stumbled and splashed, his hands full of big rocks. Now we had him trapped between us like a baseball player trying to steal a base. We shouted and threw more rocks and made a colossal racket and I'm glad no Indians were watching.

The agouti was running short on breath, either from laughing at us or from trying to get away from us. When I finally got a direct hit on its back, it stopped swimming long enough to come up for air, right under where B.C. stood perched on a huge boulder, sort of like a big vulture. B.C. was too shot to be dramatic — he just more or less dropped his rock on the agouti's head and that was that. Exhausted, we hauled it to shore, gutted it, helped each other pick up our packs and slogged on. Fortunately our guides were waiting for us just around the bend and they were delighted to carry the agouti. We were delighted to let them.

Somehow we made it to Monte Carmelo that night. B.C.'s toes were ground into raw meat by all the sand he'd gotten in his shoes and my feet were blistered from having to wear shoes at all. My special sister Antonina fed us a supper of macaroni and pancakes and fried eggs and papaya and I'm sure B.C. thought he'd died after all and was surprised to find that the angels had black hair. I'd known all along they would.

In the end, B.C. lost 47 pounds and Mrs. C. thought he looked pretty good when he got back, not that she recognized him at first, what with his pants wrapped around twice and his shirt just sort of dangling off what used to be his shoulders.

In fact, when I saw them recently, B.C. was looking definitely rounder and Mrs. C. whispered something along the lines of would I be willing to take him on another airstrip project. She would arrange to drop the food in the river, she said.

# Chapter 5

## *Getting Around*

My friend Itch and I were both scared but because he was fifteen and I was fourteen, we would never admit it. "Itch" was Phil Eichenberger, the doctor's son. We sat in a 26-foot dugout canoe on the Urubamba River, him in front and me in back, racing through a coal-black night at 9 p.m. in a dense fog. We could hear the frightening roar of a rapid up ahead but we had no idea which way to go to get through it.

Suddenly a massive tree, stuck in the rapid, materialized thirty feet in front of us.

"Let's get to the right," I shouted. We

rowed furiously, our long paddles banging on the shallow rocks. In seconds we had swept past the tree and knew we were lucky. But now we were sideways to the current and the canoe started banging on rocks.

"Which way is the current headed?" Itch called back.

"I can't tell," I answered, but we've got to get straightened out or we're gonna roll."

Flipping the fully-loaded canoe in the dark with no idea what was up ahead didn't have any appeal at all, especially since we didn't have life jackets or lights. We tried to regain control, but it was all too confusing.

"Let's jump out," I finally suggested desperately. "We've got to get slowed down." Itch and I went overboard simultaneously. The cold swift water tore at our legs and the rocks pinched our toes, but we hung onto the canoe with iron grips.

Once we were straight with the current we slowly, carefully walked the canoe down through the rapid, splashing water into it the whole way. Finally when we couldn't touch the bottom anymore, we clambered in, soaked and shivering. The canoe, free of our restraint, charged off into the thick white cloud, toward more rapids, toward more logs stuck in the river. We couldn't see either shore, couldn't see where we were going, could barely see each other.

Itch and I were on a 14-day canoe trip from

Camisea to Pucallpa and we knew it could be dangerous. "Over my dead body," our mothers had said when we asked for permission to do it. "Sure, if you can get a good canoe," our fathers had said. We got a good canoe.

We had asked the Machis for tips and pointers, especially about traveling at night.

"Don't do it until you get past Bolognesi," the Machis had said. "Before that the river is too dangerous."

"What does Bolognesi look like?" we asked.

The Machis had tried to describe the town, and earlier in the day we'd been certain we'd passed it. Six days into our trip we were getting tired of the hot sun and our slow progress, so after a mosquito-infested supper on a sand bar we had decided to do our first all-night drift.

We'd agreed to take turns keeping watch — two hours on duty and two hours to sleep. We hadn't foreseen that it would be like trying to sleep in a wet bathtub that tipped and bounced whenever it banged into trees or rocks. Sleep, in fact, was rather out of the question — neither of us wanted to spend our last night on earth asleep.

Though we had already weathered some serious rapids in our overloaded canoe, sometimes even jumping out and swimming alongside to steady it when it filled with water, I wondered for the first time if we were in over our heads. I had spent a lot of time in dugouts in my life and could handle most anything the Machis could, but it was different when I couldn't see where to go.

Somehow we survived the night, dodging obstacles at the last minute and leaning to balance the canoe when it banged sideways into trees. Stiff, exhausted and frozen, we welcomed the sun as it rose over the jungle, and dozed like alligators in its warmth. Five hours later we pulled into a little town to buy some soda pop.

"What's the name of this place?" Itch asked curiously.

"Bolognesi," answered the store keeper.

"Oh," said Itch, looking at me through bleary eyes. "No wonder." Sure enough, the next night we only banged into a few trees, and even the guy on watch fell asleep. We'd both wake up to find that we'd gotten stuck on a sandbar and didn't know it until the mosquitoes found us.

We spent a lot of time goofing around in dugout canoes, both in the Machi area and at Lake Yarinacocha, but they weren't our only way of getting around. At Yarinacocha, most of us started high school with some sort of bicycle. "Some sort" means they often weren't exactly what you think of as a bicycle.

Phil Hocking, who we called "Flop" had a bike that went to the extreme. About all it had was two wheels and a frame. Since Flop's parents were with another mission, he lived in a little town a couple miles from our linguistic center and he rode his bike to school through dust or mud with no handle bars, no seat and sometimes no pedals or brakes. He could even carry his books on his head while he rode.

Terry and I had Monarchs that weighed a ton but were strong as bulls. We could smash the front wheel and give ourselves concussions and that frame would still be there for us when we came around.

One of our favorite Sunday afternoon pastimes was playing bicycle tag. There wasn't much that beat the excitement of racing down dirt roads, short cutting through people's back yards, jumping ditches, banging into each other, ducking clothes lines and even racing under the school's trapeze rings to grab hold and swing out of reach, leaving the sturdy bicycle to roll down the hill and crash into the wall of Uncle Jim's craft shop.

In those days we had coaster brakes so we could slam on the brakes and do 360 degree turns. Not that all of our bikes had brakes, of course. Since we lived some distance from good parts stores and since we didn't have to endure a hundred rules about helmets, protective pads and safety equipment, sometimes we got along quite well without brakes. If you really needed to stop, which wasn't very often in a game of tag, all you had to do was press your foot against the front wheel. If you were barefoot, which we always were, it could hurt a bit, especially if your foot got wedged up in the fork. Kids who had bikes without brakes usually had calluses with grooves in them.

One of the first things the Indians wanted to do when they came to our center was to learn how to ride a bicycle. After some wobbly rides and lots of crashes, they'd learn how to go, never thinking that they'd sooner or later have to stop. I remember seeing a Campa man flying down a long hill, black hair blowing, black eyes glowing. Since it was a Sunday afternoon, I knew that the airstrip gate at the bottom of the hill was closed, but he didn't. In seconds, sure enough there was a splintering crash and a long silence.

Fortunately the bike and the embarrassed man were both hardy. After I'd helped sort out what parts were bicycle and what parts were Indian, I tried to show him how the brakes worked, but he still didn't think they were all that important.

"I should have jumped off sooner," he said in broken Spanish. Never mind that he was going 20 miles an hour.

About the time I turned 15 everything changed. That's when my dad and a few other wild-eyed fanatics bought motorcycles. Hondas were making a dramatic entry into the jungle and Dad was never one to be last in line. We eagerly drove to Senor Vargas' fabulous Pucallpa showroom and bought a Honda 90. We couldn't imagine anything more beautiful, more powerful, more... uhh... useful in our parents' ministry.

At least the 90 was more powerful than Beasley's 50, which wasn't much more than a bicycle with makeup. Every Saturday morning Uncle Dave and Aunt Nancy Beasley went shopping in Pucallpa on that pitiful thing, with tall lanky Uncle Dave driving and portly Aunt Nancy sitting side saddle on what was left of the seat after Uncle Dave got his share. Meaning she sort of hung off the back. At every hill Uncle Dave would have to help out the motorcycle, leaning forward and pushing with his long legs until the engine could make it on its own again. Rumor had it that Uncle Dave never changed the oil because he didn't think it was wise to be tearing into the engine like that all the time.

Anyway, Terry and I were very grateful for our 90, since we thought it would be a little humiliating to have a motorcycle that you had to walk up hills, especially with girlfriends half hanging off the back.

Not that the Honda 50 was the wimpiest

cycle on the center. For some reason the Jenkins boys ended up with a genuine moped, complete with pedals. That *had* to be a donation from some church group.

The Jenks boys overcame its lame image by learning how to do wheelies on it, which was the ultimate test of a cycle's usefulness.

With the coming of motorcycles, turning 15 meant coming of age. Our center didn't have many rules about motorcycles at the start — they added a bunch more when my sisters Sandy and Melody learned to drive, especially after Sandy ran over two of our center directors — but you had to be 15 to drive one by yourself and there was a speed limit that no one knew or followed except for some of the older ladies who stuck to the speed limit because they never figured out how to shift out of first gear.

Motorcycles became our joy and sport. We went on camping trips with two people and a ton of gear on each cycle, sometimes driving seven or eight hours on muddy roads in pouring rain. We learned to trade drivers across two cycles while still weaving down the road. We cruised the center with four teens on a Honda 90. We discovered that if the passenger sat backward, he could pull a wagon or lawnmower or baby stroller, or even carry a 55-gallon barrel on his lap if the driver didn't start off too fast.

During lunch breaks from school Towner

and I raced buses on the road to Pucallpa, often rocketing along behind them completely blinded by clouds of dust and finally passing just hoping no one was coming from the other direction.

Almost everyone owned Hondas with automatic clutches, but my first scooter was a Lambretta with a manual clutch. When Towner taught me to drive it I didn't have a clue how clutches worked. I started at the bottom of a hill in front of Towner's house, let out the clutch and went roaring off without any idea what to do next. Totally out of control, I raced through a clump of lemon grass bushes, bounced over an embankment, dropped into a ditch and dove over the handlebars while the engine died. Towner swears he was yelling "pull in the clutch" the whole time, but I never heard a thing.

Sandy was even worse when I taught her to drive. She figured she already knew everything there was to know about motorcycles, so it pretty much boiled down to me getting on the back while she got in front. She gave it full throttle and then, to her everlasting credit, she jumped off just before we smashed into our shed. I didn't.

Sandy still drives that way — the last motorcycles we bought together were Honda 450s in Texas. She's short enough that her feet didn't quite reach the ground,

so as often as not she'd fall over at red lights
and have to get passing motorists to help
her get going again.

The roads and the jungle and especially
the drivers were hard on those motorcycles
and sooner than we wished they started
falling apart. Not that the engines ever quit
running — there just wasn't much left for
them to push. Within a few years it was
amazing how so many dangling bits and
pieces could still roll down the road with
people on them.

Headlights fell out, side lights broke off,
shock absorbers clanked and banged and
bottomed out, speedometers stuck at
various speeds, worn bearings gave the
steering a wobbly feel, ignition locks were
replaced with hot wires, shift and brake
levers got bent into "S" and "Z" and other
alphabetic shapes. Worst of all, engines got
hard to start, so it wasn't unusual to see
friends pushing their cycles for miles trying
to induce a sputter or a cough. My record
push was four miles and it never did start,
but I remained optimistic throughout,
never stopping until it was time for lunch.

Lucky Terry got his hands on an old
Triumph 500 for a while. It didn't run for
more than a couple of days at a time, since
the closest place to get parts was Miami, but
when it ran it was thunder and lightning
and tornadoes. More than one person

climbed on, hit the throttle and got thrown right off the back. Just having that thing in our yard was pretty heady stuff, even when it wasn't running.

I don't remember when or why we decided to move on to horses. We certainly didn't need them for getting around, but somehow it seemed a good idea. Maybe we were inspired by Itch, who read every Western that made it to Peru and talked Western and had a horse named Chestnut and a donkey named Brighty. Chestnut was tolerable, but Brighty was even noisier than my dad in the mornings, and what with the fact that we only had screen windows on our houses he didn't last long. Brighty, I mean. Not that we didn't have neighbors who wished they could ship Dad off with the donkey some mornings.

There was a huge cattle ranch about fifty miles from our center. One Sunday afternoon we chartered a rattly old truck and drove out to buy three horses. Terry got pregnant Brownie, our friend Randy got Carachi and Towner got Tiny.

Unfortunately I already had a little horse by then, so I didn't get a chance at a good one. Mine was Blaze, but about the only thing that blazed in her was her temper. If I said giddap she put her head down and grabbed a big mouthful of grass. If I gently kicked her in the ribs she whipped her head back and grabbed a big mouthful of my bare toes. If I swatted her with the reins she bucked until I stopped.

Blaze's basic training came from Dad, who fancied himself a horse breaker since he'd ridden a little on the farm when he was young. We used a pretty sophisticated method: one of us stood behind Blaze, and when Dad kicked her in the ribs we whacked her on the backside with a 2x4. We used a long 2x4 because once when Terry and I were putting her bridle on she tried to bite me. I slapped her hard on the nose and she spun around and got Terry right in the stomach with both hind hooves, which he didn't think was fair.

The best thing you could say for Blaze was that she was pretty and when she was in the mood she was fast. She was seldom in the mood. Most of our races ended up with me either dangling from her neck or sitting on the ground, since we rode bareback and she had a terrible habit of either screeching to a halt or making a U-turn whenever I urged her to speed up. I usually couldn't stop or turn as fast as she could.

Towner's Tiny wasn't tiny. He was enormous, like a huge black draft horse. Towner's biggest problem with Tiny was getting on him, sort of like trying to climb onto a propane tank on stilts. I think Tiny had something loose inside, because when he trotted or galloped it sounded like everything was sloshing around, sort of like a live rock tumbler. He was gentle and kind, but a little stupid. He'd stand on Towner's feet and never know it until Towner slugged him in the gut. Towner hit him so hard once he broke his finger, but Tiny just swished his tail and kept chewing, happy for the attention.

I called Itch not long ago to reminisce about the horses.

"Remember that time we hitched Chestnut to the farm wagon and rode into Pucallpa for a load of rice hulls?" he asked.

"Umm..." I said, not remembering but not wanting to stifle him either.

"We tied up in front of El Rincon and there was that skinny old horse tied in the alley beside the restaurant, kind of leaning against the wall."

"Errrr..." I mumbled, warming to the story and wishing I could remember so I could put it in my book with a clear conscience. We did eat at El Rincon, a greasy little restaurant, pretty often.

"We went inside to order and before our food came a guy staggered in carrying a big hunk of fresh meat, still dripping blood." Itch liked those kinds of earthy details, even if you don't.

"Uhhhhh..." I continued, guessing what

was coming.

"When we finished, we went back outside to get our wagon and the only thing left of that nag in the alley was a big pile of bones and guts. Best steak we ever had at the Rincon."

Suddenly it all came back to me, though I'm almost positive I wasn't there.

It really doesn't have anything to do with this story, but I might as well add that Terry's Queenie eventually gave birth to a cute white colt. Melody claimed him and proudly named him King. He eventually grew from a cute colt to a homely white rack of ribs whose most outstanding feature was his lower lip. It was about the size of a salad plate and it flapped and banged and oozed green saliva when he ran. Given his skinny neck and huge head, I often thought Jester would have been a better name than King, and I imagine when he died some kid cut that lip off and used it for a Frisbee.

I suppose I should mention that sometimes we even walked to some places, but that was usually a last resort after a vehicle had broken down or a road was impassable.

Probably the worst hike we ever took was to Tournavista, an agricultural experimentation station about sixty miles away, where our friend Terry Keith lived. After rain made the clay road impassable, Itch,

Terry, Terry Keith and I gave up on vehicles and set out on foot.

Using our jeans as carrying straps for our suitcases, we walked barefoot in our underwear through sticky ankle-deep red clay in the rain all day. We gnawed on really bad jerky made from smoked monkey meat, drank water from mud puddles, slept on the floor of a thatched hut and swam across flooded creeks when the bridges were out. By the time we arrived at the Keiths' house, we had walked close to thirty miles.

After a week of hunting alligators and ducks, floating down a river on giant inner tubes, eating Mrs. Keith's fabulous cooking and recuperating from our walk in, we did it all over again to get home.

About the only really fun thing about the hike was slogging along chewing on a smoke-blackened monkey arm with the hand dangling from my mouth, which made people take a second look if nothing else.

Apart from the canoes, bicycles, motorcycles, horses and our legs, the only other way to get around was by public transportation, which sounds boring by comparison but wasn't. The buses that ran between Yarinacocha and Pucallpa were far and away the greatest risks we ever took. You never knew when an engine might blow up, or a huge piece would fall off, or you'd drop through the floorboards because you had so much dust in your eyes you couldn't see where you were stepping. They were always pretty crowded, so you had to deal with pickpockets, sweaty bodies and passengers that threw up on you instead of out the window.

Usually somewhere along the way a blind man would get on with a homemade instrument and start shouting and scraping, which is a more accurate description than singing and strumming. Lots of people gave him coins so he'd get off and go to the next bus. Kids clawed their way down the aisles to sell Chiclets, the radio blared, passengers pushed and shoved.

There were special days when people celebrated by mixing mud with black ink and throwing it through the windows, none of which closed. Fortunately they threw buckets of dirty water in too, so if you were lucky you could wash the mud off without getting out of your seat. Bus rides were definitely not boring.

We seldom went to Lima, but when we did the best entertainment was riding collectivos around the city at night.

"Whaddya wanna do?" I'd ask.

"Let's go ride a collectivo," Towner would suggest.

"You sure?"

"Sure."

Some of the people who read my last book wrote to say that our parents didn't take very good care of us. They're about to think that again. In defense of my parents I have to say that back then it didn't seem all that stupid to let your teens go roaring off late at night in an unsafe vehicle through a city that had one of the highest accident rates in the world. At least back then there weren't terrorists or drug thugs.

Collectivos were like taxis, but they ran a specified route and collected passengers along the way. To hail one, you'd stand on a street corner and watch for a car coming with the driver's hand stuck out the window. He'd have 1-5 fingers sticking up to let you know how many empty seats he had, and if you were a match you climbed in, usually over the top of someone who wanted to keep his window seat. Very early in life you learned to close the door gently to keep it from falling off. From this point on you were kind of a prisoner because there usually weren't door handles on the inside. Not that you couldn't just climb out through a broken window.

The thing that made it fun was that collectivo drivers lived their short lives in a perpetual race, always wanting to get ahead of every other collectivo driver so they could pick up the next available passengers. The drivers were almost always sleepy from putting in long days collecting a nickel per passenger and their cars were almost always antiques, unrestored.

Wires dangled from everywhere, there were holes in the floorboards, steering wheels only vaguely worked the wheels, gear shifts growled and ground. Often there were no lights, no knobs or buttons, no dashboards to speak of. There was never a seat belt, but always a picture of a saint or a crucifix hanging from the rearview mirror, which some would say provided better protection than seat belts without the extra cost and maintenance.

To get started we all held our breath until the clutch quit shaking the whole car. To get stopped we held our breath until the driver had pumped the brakes enough to slow us down.

Collectivo drivers were geniuses at negotiating crowded streets, dodging pedestrians, getting onto and off of sidewalks at full speed, running red lights, shifting and steering with their right hand while loudly banging their left hand on the outside of their door — it was illegal to use horns in the city — and passing each other the wrong way on one-way streets. An hour in a collectivo was always a good reminder that it's great to be alive, and at 5 cents per ride it was certainly cheaper than going bowling. But would I let my sons do it?

Not unless they invited me to go along.

# Chapter 6

## *The Shot*

The smiling nurse at our little clinic nodded encouragingly as I aimed a used hypodermic needle at a green orange. She was quite sure I could do it just right, though I couldn't help but notice that she offered me an orange to practice on instead of her own much more realistic skin.

"It feels a lot like the real thing," she said again. "You kind of jab with the needle first, then you'll have to push a bit to get it through the hard part. After that it goes in easy." I kind of jabbed, pushed a bit and injected the orange with a shot of sterile water that it didn't particularly need.

"Great!" exclaimed the nurse, acting as if I'd just saved the citrus. "Now when you do the real thing, you'll sort of mentally divide one of your patient's buns into quarters, and you'll aim for the upper outside quadrant. That'll keep you away from important nerves and veins." I mentally divided my little orange, thinking that a cantaloupe or a gourd would probably be closer to the size of a Machiguenga's bun.

"Don't be afraid to shove the needle all the way to the hilt, then pull back a bit on the plunger. If you see blood coming into the syringe, just yank out the needle and shoot again."

*Yeah right*, I thought. *Like I'm going to stand there all day poking and jabbing at some poor dying Indian's upper outside quadrant in search of blood-free muscle. If I wanted to play darts, I wouldn't use my friends' backsides.* But because I was fourteen, I didn't let on that the sight of blood in my syringe might leave me woozy, and she was so enchanted with my success that she didn't notice my face turning pale.

The shot lessons were part of my training to be my mother's official partner in Camisea for the summer. In fact, they were about all the training I got. Dad had taken on some administrative duties that kept him desk bound at Yarinacocha and

our organizational policy wouldn't allow
Mom to go so far from help for two months
without a partner to handle emergencies.
Some of you might think that I would be the
greatest source of her emergencies, but in
their greater wisdom our directorate said
that if I could operate the radio and give
shots, I was as good as Dad.

At the time, Dad and Mom were deeply
into linguistic and literacy work, so they
both wanted Mom to get some time in a
village. My job would be to upgrade the
airstrip, teach literacy classes, keep our
aging hut lashed together, take care of
Sandy and Melody and help make sure that
no one in my family or the rest of village
died. Sounded like fun to me. Terry went to
be Bob Tripp's partner in an Amarakeri
village for the summer, doing roughly the
same things I was but without sisters.
Lucky guy.

Shots basically boiled down to penicillin,
and nobody thought penicillin shots were
fun. The stuff itself is so thick it takes a
large-bore needle roughly the size of a
12-gauge shotgun, and once it's injected it
makes a bulge that leaves you feeling for
several hours as if you've got a full wallet in
your hip pocket. Not that any of us would
have known back then what a full wallet felt
like.

I got penicillin shots about as often as we

got rain during rainy season, not that the two are at all related. Except of course that the little buggers that cause infections probably go crazy in the humidity.

All I had to do to get a good infection was nick myself with the tip of my jackknife. If I was lucky, I could hide the oozing and swelling until that part of my body just fell off. Otherwise my temp would climb like a Machi kid going after papayas, telltale red streaks would run like paths to the closest lymph node, and I'd get another series of seven bun-busting penicillin shots. I can't figure out why a little nick would go all festery but the huge holes the needles made never did, and I think it's unfair that kids nowadays have so many options including oral antibiotics. If today's teens had to get penicillin shots, they'd behave better. All we'd have to say is, "If you don't straighten up, I'm gonna give you a shot," which is what the Machis told their kids.

The good thing was that we learned as infants just where all our lymph nodes were, since they swelled up when we got infections. Kids nowadays don't even know what a lymph node is unless they happen to be paying attention that day in biology class.

We arrived in Camisea around noon and went to work sweeping and tying. There were always piles of droppings left by bats and crickets and mice that lived in the thatch over our heads. Sort of a welcome mat letting us know that we were back among friends. In spite of our joy at being reunited with them, we hung mosquito nets to keep their nocturnal droppings and drippings off our faces and to keep malaria mosquitoes from shortening our stay.

The Coleman lantern leaked air and the Primus stove leaked gas and the roof leaked rain. Andres the school teacher dropped in to let us know that a good wind would probably blow the whole house over, since most of the vines that held it together had worn out. He didn't offer any particular solution to the problem, and probably only said it so that Mom wouldn't sleep at night, in which case her linguistic work would progress faster.

The first night we stayed awake to the chatter of all the animals and insects that were griping about the smoke from our log fire. The second night Mom and I were wakened by a family whose baby was dying. In fact, the tiny little boy died in our house in the middle of the night, by the light of a kerosene lamp. His mother softly wailed as she and his father disappeared back into the darkness.

I had just one person in my literacy class: Navidad, the ever eager father of our good friend Spider Monkey. Navidad's nicely carved mahogany face faithfully showed up every time someone was willing to teach him, but his progress was slow. Everyone in our family claims to have taught him how to read and we probably all did. He easily forgot everything between teachers.

We lay side by side on the palm floor of our house, with me pointing my finger at Machiguenga syllables and helping Navidad to pronounce them.

"Ah," I'd say, pointing to an "A."

"Ah," Navidad would repeat as if he knew that A stood for Ah, which he didn't.

"Pa," I'd continue, confident that soon he'd be able to combine two syllables into his first word.

"Pa," he'd repeat, and we'd go through it all again until I was sure he had it. "Ah... pa...ah...pa...ah...pa..." faster now "ah pa ah pa ah pa" pointing back and forth and watching "apa" come together in glorious fusion.

"Now," I'd say in my most encouraging voice, which wasn't very encouraging after the twentieth attempt, "look at these two syllables together." Right before our eyes, in stunningly clear letters, we could both see "Apa." The difference was that whereas I could see the word for "father," Navidad couldn't say for sure what he was seeing.

"What does it say?"

Navidad would grimace, stutter, tense

up, try a few things that didn't sound anything like Apa, and then give up with a sad look into my eyes.

I loved Navidad dearly and still do, but I wished fervently that I could just inject a bucketful of literacy into his buns instead of torturing him day after day. Although he eventually got to the place where he could put Ah and pa together to make apa, he never could easily read the Scriptures, which was what motivated him to work so hard at it. He loved God, and loved the newly translated Bible portions. Now that both my mom and I are over forty and can't read either, we wonder, sadly, if all he really needed was a good pair of glasses.

While I struggled on with Navidad, building more patience than literacy, my mother taught women's classes on our front porch, where a dozen women in cushmas sprawled with their nursing babies. It was about as motley a class as ever gathered, but by the time those babies got to high school, a higher percentage of Machis would be literate than Americans, though it was pretty hard to imagine that at the time.

Fixing an airstrip by hand isn't as fun as it sounds but at least I could see more progress than I could with Navidad. Besides, it was a lot easier than building one from scratch like I'd done in Kompi. Camisea had a long, grassy airstrip but it had a ridge running diagonally across the middle of it. We thought it was pretty fun, since you did a kind of belly dropping roller coaster plunge during takeoff. The pilots, whose imaginations were limited by their technical training, weren't quite as thrilled with it and wanted us to taper the ridge off to a more gentle slope.

Since the airstrips were our lifelines, allowing us to get everything from medicines to mail, we pretty much tried to do whatever the pilots asked. These days, of course, I wouldn't touch that job with less than a tractor and a dump truck, but since I had a deprived childhood, back then I thought everyone moved dirt with a shovel and a burlap bag.

Most mornings I got up in the cool predawn fog to claw off a bit more dirt with a pickax. Once a little pile had accumulated, I'd carefully shovel it into the bag until it was too heavy to carry but still light enough to drag. Then I'd drag it down to a low spot and dump it. Our packer was a short section of log with two upright handles tied to it, and that thing was a shoulder builder if ever there was. People could save a lot of money on fitness centers if they'd just spend a couple hours each morning packing airstrips.

I thought my dawn and dusk diligence would inspire Machis to come join me, but they took the more sensible approach that as long as I was working so hard, they didn't need to and besides, I didn't have a garden to take care of. If you talk to Sandy and Melody, they'll claim to have helped, but don't believe a word of it. They couldn't even pick up the log packer.

Even my own efforts ground to a halt when I machete'd my right ankle, which, as you already know, immediately led to a massive infection that bulged the lymph node in my groin. Again.

I wish I could say I cut myself working on the airstrip or doing something else of eternal value, but that would be a lie and an exaggeration and there aren't any lies or exaggerations in my books, even if Terry thinks that's about all they are. In any case, at the time I was hacking a pair of water skis out of balsa logs. For a long time I'd watched how fast the water raced down through the rapid that nearly killed Terry and me on the log ride I wrote about in my first book, and I got this idea that if I could just fasten a rope to something and swing out into the current, I could ski.

Sculpting water skis with a machete isn't particularly easy, so I used balsa, figuring it would be softer to cut and the added buoyancy couldn't hurt. I was doing the final trimming, holding down one end of a ski with my foot and thinking that if the machete bounced I'd cut my ankle, when sure enough it bounced and I proved myself right.

Blood flowed freely all over the beautiful white wood, infectious bugs whooshed in from all directions, and I ended up getting another 12 gauge shot. This time it was from a passing pilot who was a little concerned that my feverish protests didn't make sense. I think Mom was so used to me not making sense that she didn't pick up on it right away. Anyway I was really lucky that the pilot happened to be passing through and had some newfangled formulation in his medical kit that only required one shot instead of the normal seven. I love that man!

Although this story isn't about the water skiing, I suspect you'll want to know what happened so you can try it yourself. If you're not the adventurous type, skip this section. If you're the adventurous type but you only like to read success stories, you can skip this section too. If you're the type that thinks it's better to have tried and failed than never to have tried, let's form a support group.

I can't say that my skis were perfect, but they were pretty good. They were about six feet long and pretty thick. Bindings would have helped, but of course I didn't have any so I tied on an old pair of tennis shoes with nylon fishing line. I was as ready as I could be.

After I'd recovered sufficiently from my ankle infection, or at least convinced Mom that I had, she steered the canoe for me while I poled up to the rapid late one afternoon. Then she stood on the bank to take pictures while I got set up. I think she always imagined that each picture of her kids might be the last.

I walked upriver a ways with a length of nylon rope, jumped in and tumbled down through the waves and over the rocks to where a log was stuck in the middle of the rapid. With more than a little effort I grabbed hold and tied one end of my rope to it, then flailed my way back to shore with the other end. By now my teeth were chattering and my muscles shivering in the shadowy cold.

Tying my feet into the tennis shoes, I assumed the water skier's crouch and side-slipped into the water, wishing for a life jacket to stabilize me. The current was pretty rough, tossing me this way and that as I swung into the turmoil below the log. Straining to keep hold of the rope, keep my feet in the shoes, keep the shoes on the skis and keep the skis roughly pointed into the current, I wrestled furiously and slowly began to stand up, a smile forming deep inside me. My shoulders lifted out... then my waist... *the thrill of victory — I would*

*be the first water skier in all of Machiguenga
land... then my knees... then... without
warning my right ski broke. The agony of
defeat.* I'm sad to say the pictures weren't
even all that great. Anyway, that's not what
this story is about, but if you ever want to
try it, find a waterfall and don't use balsa
and get good bindings and at least do it
when there's enough light for pictures.

Mom's and my first big medical case of
the summer was a teenage girl named Rosa
who fell out of the rafters in her house and
broke her collar bone. By the time she
arrived at our house her eyes were wide
with fear, thinking she would die soon.

Having never fixed a broken collar bone
before, we got on the radio and talked to Dr.
Eichenberger about it. It turned out that
the treatment was pretty simple: put a knee
between her shoulder blades, pull her
shoulders back to let the ends of the bones
come together, take an ace wrap and make
a tight figure eight around her shoulders to
keep everything properly positioned for a
few weeks.

Although it now seems simple, and I
could fix your fractured collarbone for a
fraction of what your doctor would charge,
at the time we were getting our instructions
through all the static of the universe, and
we got it a little wrong. We didn't get the
knee between the shoulder blades part

quite right and we put the figure eight on across her chest instead of her back and we're both glad Rosa didn't know anything about malpractice suits. It probably didn't help that I was fourteen and she was thirteen and I was trying to do it all without looking at her.

The good news is that Rosa didn't die, which she wouldn't have anyway. She did end up with a bit of a bony bump on that collarbone, since we didn't get the ends quite together. I wish I had a souvenir like that — she didn't even appreciate how lucky she was.

And now for the shot. Late one afternoon a girl came to our house. "Can you help my brother?" she asked quietly. "He has an infection on his leg." Mom asked a couple of questions and looked my way.

"Why don't *you* give him a penicillin shot? He'd probably rather get shot by you than by me." Although I could follow the reasoning, since the sick boy was about my age, I thought I'd probably forego a bit of modest embarrassment in order to get my shot from someone who knew what she was doing. But then the boy didn't know this would be my first effort, so what did it matter?

I thought a lot about the green orange while we sterilized a used needle in a black kettle of boiling water over our smoky cook

fire. It had been a few weeks since I'd had
my training and I hadn't shot anything
since. Mom reviewed some cautions and
reminders and I was off in search of the
kid's bloodless upper outer quadrant.

The boy lay on his side on the front porch
of his hut. He looked feverish and
miserable. A nasty cut on his leg had gone
wildly septic, oozing and swelling. I asked
about pain in his groin, and he showed me
where the lymph node on the left side had
abscessed to the size and shape of his pinky
finger. I shuddered inside while I asked him
to roll over so I could give him the shot. He
groaned audibly as he rolled, and I groaned
inwardly.

I had no problem pulling his shorts down
a bit. No problem dividing the left bun into
quarters, having always been good at
geometry. No problem swabbing the upper
outside quadrant with a cotton ball
dripping with alcohol. But when it came to
actually purposely stabbing someone I
knew in the backside with a needle… well…
I have to admit my stomach was knotting
and churning and I was probably feeling
sicker than he was.

I took careful aim for several long
seconds while he tensed, endlessly waiting,
then jabbed. The needle sort of bounced. He
winced and went "huunnnhhh" with what I
was sure was his last breath. My own

stomach convulsed and my knees went wobbly and I couldn't get the needle to go in. Just like a green orange. Right. The cheerful nurse should have had me practice on a rhinoceros rump.

There was nothing to do but try again. I smeared more alcohol all over the place, braced myself, took careful aim and jabbed again. He shuddered again and went "huunnnhhh" again and I shoved again with no more luck than last time. I could tell he wasn't impressed. I wasn't even impressed.

"Third time's the charm," I muttered to myself even though I wasn't at all sure that it would be. What had been a sort of miserable boy on the front porch was now a pathetically more miserable boy with big question marks added to the pain in his eyes. I swabbed again, braced again, jabbed again. "Huunnnhh," he said. Each time he winced, of course, his leg twitched and his swollen lymph node sent shots of pain everywhere, as I knew only too well. I pushed as hard as I could, which wasn't very hard given my failing strength and gave up. Pulled out the needle. Walked despondently back to our house. Left the boy moaning and writhing on his porch.

"Okay, I'll give it a try," Mom said when I gave her my dismal report. She wasn't quite as ready as I was just to let him die because he had a leather backside.

Off we went, mother and son, to spend some quality time together. I can't imagine that Sandy and Melody wouldn't have come along too, as much as they loved watching pain and misery in progress. Still, I don't remember them being there, which may just be because I have tried to forget the whole thing.

This time the boy winced and went "huunnnhhh" just seeing me. The relief was obvious when he realized that Mom held the syringe. She swabbed him yet again, giving him the most sterile shot spot in the whole Amazon basin. She took aim in seconds and made a swift, practiced jab. She'd gotten her practice on me, of course, but never mind that. The boy winced and went "huuunnnhhh" for the fourth time.

"Boy!" she said. "This guy's got tough skin." By now his skin had enough holes in it that it should have been like giving a shot to a sponge, but even she couldn't get the needle to push in. She pulled it out for a close look.

"You know, I think this needle has a burr on it," she said with squinty eyes. "We're going to have to file it off when we get home." *Great*, I thought. *For my very first shot I get a needle with no point.*

"Well... we've got to get it in somehow," she said finally. And with that she swabbed again, jabbed with a ferocity that gave me new respect for her latent aggressions, and pushed with both hands. The boy looked like he'd actually been hit by a 12 gauge shotgun. The palm floor shook and he writhed and she shoved and I wobbled and the needle went to the hilt, tearing a tunnel through the tissue the whole way in.

When she pulled back on the plunger to check for blood, I fully expected to see a fountain of it, given the way things had been going, but thankfully she'd hit pure muscle. Thank God for that!

It took a minute or so to get all of the penicillin in, and then with a violent yank Mom pulled the needle back out and the boy's leg jerked and the house shook for the last time and it was over.

The boy recovered nicely from both the infection and the shots, though for a long time whenever he drank water his upper outer quadrant leaked like a sprinkler. And he always trembled when he saw me coming.

At the end of the summer, Navidad could say "apa" on cue, no matter what syllables I was pointing at. The next pilot who flew to Camisea walked the length of the airstrip, pronounced it a major improvement and handed me about twenty dollars for my summer's work. I didn't even get to use the strip — by that time, I'd talked Mom and Dad into letting me go back to Yarina by canoe with Itch, my fifteen-year-old friend. Itch flew out to join me for the trip and the Machis couldn't quite figure out why we'd trade a safe two-hour ride in a plane for a dangerous two-week ride in a dugout canoe, but that's just because they take their great opportunities for granted.

In case you're wondering, I've never given another penicillin shot. I probably never will.

# Chapter 7

## *Our Hut*

For this chapter, you'll need some imagination, so just close your eyes as you read. If you think that's impossible, you should have seen some of the students in my Machiguenga literacy classes. Remember Navidad? Whenever I asked him to read he'd scrunch his eyes shut and search frantically for any word that he thought I might be pointing at. With his superb memory, he'd usually come up with it, though it could easily take a few dozen tries.

Anyway, picture yourself lying on your back on the floor of our village house. Ignore

the things that are squawking, barking
quacking and laughing under the floor.
Ignore also the fact that the whole floor
shakes whenever anything happens
anywhere else in the house. Like Sandy
hiccuping at the far end, or Melody giggling
while she's cutting her hair with a butcher
knife, or Chico the Chihuahua trotting from
one flea scratch to the next, generating 9.5
on the Richter scale. For some reason
known only to physicists, a trotting dog sets
up a resonating rhythm that could pretty
much knock the house down.

Lying on your back looking up at the roof,
you're especially glad to have your eyes
closed. That's because all sorts of stuff kind
of floats and drips and drops down from the
thatched roof. There's general dust from the
decaying palm leaves, fine brown dust from
the bugs that are eating right through the
main beams in the house, fine white dust
from the DDT residue that coats the whole
house when the malarial prevention teams
come through once a year, bat droppings
and bits of bugs that the spiders spit out.

Thatched roofs are beautiful. There are
several different kinds of palm leaves that
Machis use and they each form their own
special pattern when they're tied on to the
web of rafters and stringers. The best leaves
are naturally the ones that are the farthest
away and hardest to get. They grow on a

short bush and are shaped like a long chevron and it takes eons to collect enough to thatch one house. Our houses used about 14,000 leaves each, which is a lot of tromping around in the jungle with a machete.

Leaf gathering campouts downriver gave us a chance to hunt and fish in new places, even though the leaf cutting and hauling wasn't particularly interesting. I suppose the most excitement we had was the morning a sharp-eyed Machi spotted a tapir walking up the bank downriver. Tapirs love water and usually head for the river at dawn to bathe and take advantage of the flush toilet. You wouldn't want to be down stream.

Anyway, the Indians jumped into a canoe and Terry and I were quick enough to jump with them, not that we were particularly invited. Our stalking skills were legendary, meaning just the two of us could sound like a whole herd of wild pigs stampeding.

By the time we got there, the tapir had disappeared into the jungle, but in a rare stroke of good luck he had stopped to wallow, just like little kids that get all cleaned up for church and then head for a mudhole in the front yard. The tapir was enjoying his wallow so much that he didn't hear us coming, or maybe we were so noisy he thought we were a bunch of his buddies. In any case, one of the Machis got a shot off with our .22 rifle and thought it was splendid that he didn't have to use any of his own precious shotgun shells. After he was sure he'd nailed the tapir in the heart, he handed us the gun so we could each take a shot and claim to have helped kill it.

Skinning and gutting tapirs is pretty fascinating because they have hides that are about 1/2" thick. Other tribes used to take long strips of the hide, dry it in the sun, tie it to a stick and beat their wives with it. The wives claimed they didn't feel loved if they didn't get a good beating once in a while. The Machis just threw away the skin, which was always full of ticks, cleaned the guts for soup and hauled our supper to the canoe. Terry and I were of course covered with mud and blood by then — we made sure of it, and I must say it took a lot of effort to keep the blood from washing off as we waded through rapids pulling the canoe home in the afternoon.

Whatever the type of leaves used to thatch the roof, they give you the feeling that while you were lying there minding your own business, someone plopped a woven basket over you, just like you'd slam a jar down on a tarantula to catch it for a pet. Nicely woven new roofs are a joy to look at but once they've aged a bit you wonder how a roof with so many holes in it could possibly keep the rain out. During rainy season you don't have time to wonder about that — you're too busy moving yourself and your stuff around looking for a dry spot.

As soon as they could afford it the Machis started switching to metal roofs, which in the tropical heat offer all the relaxed comfort of a solar oven. Besides, since less bats and bugs live in them, you end up with nothing for your pet squirrel monkeys to eat. Still and all, a few sheets of metal are easier to lash on than 14,000 leaves, and the Machis are a very practical people.

We never had ceilings in our houses, but on at least one end we had a kind of loft where Terry and I usually got to sleep. Some people would think we were the luckiest boys in the whole world, getting to sleep in the loft like that with all of our insects and rodents and flying friends. Unfortunately, for some reason I can't remember, every loft was built above our cook fire, and in the mornings we always smelled like fresh sausages. I'm sure Terry got some medical syndrome from it. He's sure I got one.

Sandy and Melody were always begging for a chance to sleep in the loft with us. One summer Sandy and I had to share a mosquito net, with our air mattresses side by side. Every night as we fell asleep I put my arm around her, told her "I love you, Pooh," said good night and slightly unscrewed the valve to her air mattress. She thought that was the most miserable excuse for an air mattress ever made, until the day I went camping and she realized that whenever I was gone, the air mattress didn't go flat. Once she figured that out, I didn't have to tell her I loved her anymore and she thought I was the most miserable excuse for a brother ever made.

Our houses always had walls around two thirds of the living area. Since there were rather substantial cracks in the walls, they didn't actually afford much privacy and we could usually see bright black eyeballs staring at us. In about two weeks an optometrist could have examined the whole village one eye at a time without getting out of bed.

The walls pretty much defined the sleeping area. Dad and Mom and whatever kids weren't curing in the loft slept there on beds that looked like shelves and we all piled our stuff on shelves that looked like beds. The furniture was sort of a basic one-design-works-for-anything style, mostly made from skinny saplings lashed together with vines.

There were always a couple of 55 gallon barrels standing in a corner protecting books and medicines and special food treats that our parents didn't want to share with us. If Dad was lucky, there was also a big hunk of salami hanging in the rafters, as if having two sons that smelled like that wasn't enough. We learned early on that Dad loved that salami more than he loved us and nobody touched it unless they were desperate for attention. I could never quite figure out why he was so attached to that old meat when we had monkeys and tapirs and fish and macaws and insect larvae to eat. To each his own.

If you wanted privacy for changing your clothes or using the enamel potty, you yelled "Nobody look," waited a few seconds until everyone had finished looking, then did your thing fast. The only time nobody would look would be if you yelled "Everybody look." Our mosquito nets offered a bit of privacy, but during the daytime they were pretty hot since the cheesecloth they were made of didn't let a lot of air through. Besides, claustrophobics went crazy in them, as we found out when friends from the U.S. came to visit.

The front third of the house was an open porch where we had our kitchen, dining room, office, clinic, classroom, hospitality center and circus. There were almost always Indians sitting on the porch enjoying the entertainment and if we were ever alone, something was wrong.

The good thing was that the Machiguengas are unusually considerate about not being a bother and are scrupulously honest. We never had to worry about leaving things lying around in the open, no matter how precious they were. In more ways than one, our whole lives were a performance in front of a rapt audience — every move was village news within minutes.

Beyond the porch, still under the roof but down on the ground, was our cook fire, source of many delicious meals and even more that would have tasted better if we'd just eaten the firewood like the termites did. It was a little hard to control the temperature and it was a pure waste of space for a recipe to say we should bake something at 350 degrees. A range of 200-2000 degrees was about as close as we could get.

In a Machiguenga house the hearth is the heart of the home and each wife has her own for cooking and keeping warm. The fire burns all day and night and smoke fills the house. In our house our liberated mother didn't feel a deep emotional need for her own hearth, so we kids got to do all the work related to keeping it going, cooking on it and savoring it's smoke at night.

Each morning Terry and I had to grab a couple buckets apiece and head for the river to get water. It's harder than you think to carry two full buckets of water through the mud and up a steep bank without spilling it all over. If you spill it all over the trail gets slicker and you spill more and eventually you end up back in the river with the buckets on top of you.

Some of the water went immediately into a kettle that had a thick black crust on it. Then came the challenge of getting the fire going. We'd carefully roll each of our fire logs over to see if there were any live coals left. We weren't nearly as diligent as the Indians about getting up in the night to make sure the fire was still going because we had all the matches we wanted.

Still, if there was even a live coal the size of a pea we'd take special pride in not using matches. Instead we'd blow on that tiny coal just so, then lay it against some charred wood, blowing some more, adding more charred wood and kindling and eventually hyperventilating until all we could do was walk around in dizzy circles.

Sometimes on campouts the Machis thought it was more practical to just throw alcohol or kerosene on the fire to get it going, but we wanted to be like real Indians. I've seen Machis toss a handful of alcohol onto a fire only to have the flames shoot up and catch their hands on fire, which is pretty spectacular. Alcohol burns cool enough to not scorch the flesh, so no one gets very concerned and we got to see what it was like for Moses at the burning bush.

Once our fire showed signs of life, we'd alternate blowing on it and fanning it with a fan made of wild turkey feathers until it was roaring hot. Then we'd put the kettle on and settle in for a long wait until the water had boiled a full five minutes, wishing the whole time that Mom would someday reclaim her hearth.

The only redeeming thing about those waits was that we could stand holding the bottoms of our cushmas over the fire and let the warm smoky air rise right up through the neck holes. It was sort of like personalized central heating but a little more exciting because every once in a while a spark would end up against your belly button. If you've ever seen Machiguenga men dance, you know those dances got started when hot sparks bounced along their skin somewhere between their knees and necks. All they had to do was add flute music and drums.

If the water boiled before breakfast, as opposed to just before the sun went back down, I'd sometimes use the fire to cook up a batch of pancakes. I grew up loving to cook and I think that's one reason why my family was always so healthy — they say swallowing charcoal is a good way to absorb poisons in your intestines. It's really amazing how good charcoal tastes with a little boiled sugar water on it.

One Christmas Eve at Camisea we decided to celebrate with a pancake supper. We put a cast iron skillet on the fire in the middle of a thunderous rain storm, then stood around the fire shivering and coughing and blinking the smoke out of our eyes. Rain dripped through the thatch into our skillet and plates and the cold damp wind whipped right through our house and we could probably relate much better to Joseph and Mary that night than we ever could sitting in a warm church singing Deck the Halls with Boughs of Holly.

On some special occasions we'd even mix up a cake, dump the batter into the pressure cooker pot, set that into a cast iron frying pan, heap coals all around and on top of it and bake the cake for as long as we thought it might take to make it edible. That wasn't as tricky as it sounds, since in the jungle almost anything is edible.

Depending on how long it baked and how hot the coals were, we might end up with chocolate batter, or chocolate pudding, or chocolate cake, or even chocolate charcoal, and sometimes we got all four in the same pot if we were really lucky. If it wasn't even close to our expectations of real food, we could always offer it to the Machis, who didn't think anything we made was real food and so didn't have such high expectations.

One morning, in fact, a Machiguenga man sat down at our table to visit while we finished breakfast. Mom had just made up some grape jelly that didn't jell, so it was pretty watery. Now you have to understand that when you visit a Machi in his house, his wife or daughters will give you a bowl of something to drink and the only polite thing to do is to drink the whole thing in one chugalug, regardless of what you think it is. Mom put her pint of watery jelly by Maximo and you know the rest of the story. He's still wired.

Apart from our log fire, we also had a one-burner kerosene stove. You started it by pouring a little gasoline in a cup around the generator and waiting until the generator heated up so you could open the kerosene valve and pressurize it. We all learned as tiny children that if you opened the kerosene valve too soon, the whole stove would be engulfed in flames, which was more exciting than it sounds. Once the inferno died down and you pumped it up, the stove sounded like a jet engine and that's why even today every time an airplane flies over I salivate.

While I'm on gastrointestinal topics, I might as well mention that our houses only had outhouses and they weren't very fun, probably because we didn't have Sears catalogues to read. They were tiny thatched shanties with leaky roofs and big cracks in the walls and a hole in the floor boards that was so small you had to be a sharp shooter to hit it. We never had the luxury of anything to sit on because the Machis thought it would be horribly unsanitary to sit where someone else had just sat. So we had to squat on slippery boards as they did.

There just isn't any feeling in the world to compare with having to rush to the outhouse in the middle of the night in a pouring rain and hunker down to get through the low doorway only to come face to face with the biggest bug you've ever seen crawling on the rim of the hole. And the T.P. is always wet, even in the dry season, which makes you think twice about how it gets wet.

Our record outhouse catch was a weird insect with antennae eight inches long and razor sharp pincers. If you didn't have the urge to go when you walked out there you certainly did when you poked your head through the doorway and came face to face with that critter. I can't tell you how vulnerable you feel when bugs start flying and jumping around while you're squatting flat-footed in an outhouse at night.

One dreary black night in Monte

Carmelo Dad made the desperate dash to the "out." That one couldn't really be called an "outhouse" because there wasn't any house – just a hole in the ground. Dad had turned his flashlight off for privacy and was happily hurrying through his business when he heard a loud snort. He whipped around to find himself nose to nose with the village bull. Dad doesn't scare easily, but I can assure you that bull got a little more out of him.

The cows in fact didn't have any respect for our outhouses, which seldom had doors. They knocked over more than one and without shame would poke their heads in for a look or to eat the whole summer's supply of toilet paper.

One day a little Machi boy decided to run away from home, so he hid behind our outhouse. Mom went unsuspectingly to complete her daily rituals and was in the middle of her squat when she heard a sniffle. She turned around to see a bright black eyeball enjoying the show. I'm not sure that little boy is still alive. In my next book I'll tell you about the funniest outhouse the Machis ever built.

Our kitchen was pretty basic, mostly consisting of shelves that precariously held canned fruit and vegetables, plastic storage containers with teeth marks from mice in the rims, 5-gallon metal cans that held saltine crackers, cookies, powdered milk, flour, sugar and a few other staples. An assortment of smoky pots and pans hung from hooks and a little wooden box held the dishes and cutlery so DDT dust and worse things wouldn't get on them.

Although our floor was only a couple feet off the ground, there was a whole food chain under there, from the lush green moss that grew on the damp ground to the rangy roosters that crowed us awake in the mornings to the mangy dogs that snarled and snapped and fought over each crumb that fell through our floor. It was like living over a zoo. Although it wasn't a good place to be crawling around, we made frequent excursions under the house to pick up all sorts of things that had fallen through the cracks. Sometimes we'd even find little kids under there searching for treasures or getting a worm's eye view of our world.

Since we didn't have TVs and telephones, the little radio sitting on the top shelf was our only source of entertainment and contact with the outside world. The first radios were about as big as refrigerators and needed full scale generators to power them. The Machis frequently walked around the back side of them to catch a glimpse of whoever might be talking in there.

By the time I was in high school the huge

collection of tubes and wires had been transistorized into a compact single sideband transceiver powered by a 12-volt battery. Since all of SIL's radios were tuned to the same frequency, every morning at 6:50 we could entertain ourselves by listening to the other tribal teams reporting in to Yarinacocha. Not that we could always understand what they were saying.

"Thoematthhrrrenfzzzmckcktttiiiiinsls oldgpppph!" someone would shout through the static.

"Roger, got that," the radio operator would answer, leaving us all to wonder what he'd gotten. Those guys were geniuses at figuring out radio talk.

Not only did the operators have to decipher what village teams were saying, half the time they also had to translate it into reality. Since our small airplanes had to have reasonably good weather to fly, teams in the path of a flight were regularly asked for weather updates and forecasts. Those teams that desperately wanted to get their mail or fresh supplies gave noticeably better weather forecasts than those who didn't particularly care.

"There's a little fog in the treetops and a heavy dew, but it looks like it's clearing to the north," meant "the rain clouds are so thick you can't see the trees across the river and it's raining nonstop but by the time the plane gets here I'm sure there'll be a tiny little hole in the clouds so he can see where the airstrip is."

One particularly noteworthy weather report went something like, "It's 2/8 covered at 1500 feet, 8/8 covered at 2000 feet, and 3/8 covered at 3000 feet." I still wonder how that lady could see through 8/8 at 2000 to 3/8 at 3000. Radar eyes, I guess.

In addition to news and weather reports, we could listen in on everybody's shopping lists, since all supplies had to be ordered by radio. We could tell you at any given time what the toilet paper situation was in Poyeni, for example. And there were skeds with the doctor, during which linguists with embarrassing health problems would always start off with, "I've got this Indian lady on my porch who has a...." and we'd know full well she was talking about herself. There were no secrets.

So today, when I'm feeling nostalgic or homesick, I listen for the rattle of the weight on the pressure cooker, the crying of little kids whose mothers are threatening to give them shots if they don't behave, the untimely crowing of roosters at three o'clock in the morning, the quiet giggling of Indians who could never figure us out, the slap of the turkey feather fan against a glowing log, the blast furnace roar of the Primus stove, the shrill of a thousand crickets in the thatch, the crackle and buzz and overheard secrets on the radio and the quiet whisper of the air escaping from Sandy's mattress. And sometimes I long for the good old days, when the biggest problem I had was waking up in the morning smelling like a sausage.

# Chapter 8

## *Pecky-peckies and the Go-Cart*

If you've never heard a pecky-pecky engine, pause now for a moment of silent gratitude, because once peckies hit the jungle, there were no moments of silence left for gratitude or anything else.

The sound of the engine gives it its name. To get an idea, have the loudest person in your family yell at the top of their lungs "pecky pecky pecky pecky pecky" as fast as they can while you read this chapter. If you're a teacher, have the whole class do it.

If you're a pastor, have the choir do it while you're trying to preach some Sunday.

If I could pick one single technological wonder that most changed our world in the sixties, it would have to be those big black nine-horse Briggs & Stratton engines that weighed like elephants and ran like rhinos and sounded like — well, there isn't anything else that sounds like that except maybe jackhammers.

For the Indians, traditional transportation boiled down to boiling rivers. Want to visit another village? Get in a canoe. Need to go get leaves for your leaky roof? Get in a bigger canoe. Have a medical emergency that only Wayne Snell's special potions can cure? Lay the patient in the bottom of a canoe. Don't have a canoe? Chop down some small balsa logs, lash them together with a few wooden pegs and vines, climb on and spend the day up to your ankles in water.

Although the Machiguenga villages were only minutes apart in a small airplane, they were days apart by canoe — days that were one third spent in the terror of trying to keep high waves from swamping the boat on the way downriver and two-thirds spent in the tiring tedium of trying to pole and pull the canoe back upriver. Any little errand, even between the closest villages, took a day. Longer errands took weeks. On some rivers, errands took lives.

As villages grew and developed, school teachers, store keepers, pastors and health workers all needed to interact more. Airplanes helped, but it was terribly expensive to have a plane fly two hours out from Yarinacocha just for a fifteen-minute flight from a village on the Picha, for example, to a village on the Camisea. The only alternative was a three-day trip in a canoe, which we kids thought was a fabulous adventure because you got to camp out in the rain and drink hot powdered milk with sugar in it at night and hunt for turtle eggs in the sand and run skipping and jumping along the rocks while the men pulled the canoes through rapids. For whatever reasons, the Indians and our parents didn't think that was as much fun as we did.

Outboard motors helped, but not much. For one thing, they were terribly expensive. Most of the people who owned them had somehow gotten rich in the outside world or by having a bunch of Indians work for them as slaves. Besides, outboards had the huge disadvantage of always having to have their propellers deep in the water, where rocks and logs chewed them to bits in the shallow rapids.

When we were on furlough in 1963 our

home church raised the money to buy us a sparkling new 16' Shell Lake fiberglass speed boat complete with a 28 horsepower Johnson outboard. It had a short shaft on the engine so the propeller wouldn't hit so many rocks When it arrived in Peru we knew we'd solved our transportation problems for good. Until it's maiden voyage, of course, when two men from the church, including the pastor, got to see firsthand what happens when you hit a submerged rock going 18 miles an hour. The bottom of the engine disappeared.

After an eternal wait for new parts, the speedboat ended up in the deep lake at Yarinacocha, where Terry and I learned to water ski on hot Saturday afternoons and then taught everyone else in the high school to do the same on our homemade skis.

Today people tell us you can't ski with less than an 80 horsepower engine, but we even managed to ski doubles behind our 28 hardworking horses, with one of us on a slalom. All we had to do was hang on underwater for ten or fifteen minutes while the guy on doubles got up first. It was a pretty sure bet that about the time both skiers finally got up, one would fall down.

Anyway, the point of all that is that outboards didn't work too well in the shallow rivers in Machi country. Then one day a mechanical genius invented the pecky-pecky, liberating and deafening the whole world.

A pecky-pecky is like a huge lawnmower engine, except that the drive shaft comes out of the back instead of the bottom. It sits in a U-shaped cradle on a 3/4" steel pin that fits into a socket on the back of the canoe so that the engine can rock forward and backward and turn 360 degrees. Not that you'd ever want it to, since spinning it 180 degrees would put the propeller in the boat and the driver in the water. That's happened, but it isn't supposed to.

A 10-foot pipe is bolted on to the back of the engine and a drive shaft runs through the pipe to the propeller at the far end. There are steel fin-like things both over and under the propeller. The one underneath is to protect the propeller from rocks. I'm not sure what the one on top is supposed to do. Maybe it protects the propeller when the boat turns over. That happens too.

On the front of the engine there's a 3/4" steel bar about three feet long. You steer by sitting beside that bar, grabbing hold of it and using it to swivel the tail back and forth. Sometimes, as you can imagine if you're mechanically inclined and understand anything about leverages, the bar steers you. Still, the idea is simple and that's all there is to it.

That's all there is to it, I mean, until you

start the engine, which you do by lifting the propeller out of the water to reduce drag and pulling on a rope thirty or forty times while you drift backwards down through the first five rapids fiddling with various combinations of choke and throttle. The fact that pecky-peckies run forever doesn't mean they're easy to start.

Once the engine is running well enough to earn your confidence, you slowly lower the propeller into the water, sending a beautiful spray into the air until it's completely submerged and the engine stalls. Or, if you're really lucky, everything works perfectly and you begin to pick up speed.

Speed, of course, isn't exactly the right word. The engines run at just a little over a fast idle, so you wouldn't want to travel around the world with one. In fact, you wouldn't want to travel up a really rapid rapid in one, except that they are faster than poling, which you end up doing anyway. More on that later.

The genius behind the whole thing is that the propeller can be raised or lowered as the water gets deeper or shallower. Not that that's an advantage when the water is so fast and shallow that the propeller can't do anything, but at least it isn't getting chewed to bits on the rocks.

Watching a skilled motorist steer a

pecky, you begin to think that it's easy, that it's straightforward, that... well... that you could do it yourself. Eventually you ask if you can try it and you notice that all of the Machis and especially my mom are getting out of the boat.

I remember vividly the first time I tried. I grabbed hold of the tiller, lowered the prop into the water with a big smile, made a gentle turn and discovered, to my horror, that the tiller was smashing me into the side of the boat nearly knocking me overboard. It had come to life, it was evil and it was after me.

I pushed with all my might, muscles bulging and veins protruding and eventually, to my relief, the tail swung back toward center. And past center. And even further past center until I was getting pulled overboard on the other side and I was breaking my back trying to stay in the boat. That was in a calm lake.

Dad introduced the first pecky to the Machis in the late 50s and taught two men to drive it. I'm not so sure Dad was all that experienced, but that never slowed him down. When he taught Epi, they invited Mom to go along for the test run and she, unthinking, accepted. Dad sat in the front of the boat and yelled at Epi, who couldn't hear over the noise. The canoe went this way and that, banging into rocks and tipping in the strong currents and threatening to send everyone to heaven. Mom, who was ready for heaven but not quite yet, quickly panicked and got out but then couldn't get back to the village by herself. Epi had to beach the canoe, hold her hand all the way back to the village and then come back for more practice.

Going upstream in a pecky, we did everything we could to avoid the fast currents, hugging the bank and taking advantage of backwaters. Sooner or later, of course, we had to head for the fast water in the heart of the rapids. The motorist raised the rpms marginally by tightening strings and vines and the men in the front leaned into sturdy cane poles and we hoped like fury that the engine wouldn't die right there.

There was nothing quite so much fun as sitting in the middle of a raging rapid, the water rushing and roaring around us, bumping backwards on shallow rocks, the prop out of the water and the motorist trying to juggle his steering bar and a paddle. When all else failed, including sometimes the engine, we finally jumped into the torrent and just pulled the boat through, soaking ourselves and splashing water into the boat and cracking our toes in between the rocks. Other than that, going upriver was actually pretty boring.

Going downstream was never quite so boring considering the fact that the combination of the current's speed and the pecky's speed added up to some hair-raising navigation. In the worst rapids, we could actually see the river tumbling steeply downhill.

The motorist would aim into the smooth "V" of the rapid, angle carefully to the side of the biggest waves, make a sharp turn just before we hit the rocky cliff, battle the backwaters and whirlpools and burbles, and bail furiously as soon as he could get one hand free.

In the meantime, the guy in front perched precariously in the front of the bouncing canoe, jabbing with his cane pole to shove the nose this way and that around rocks that the motorist couldn't see. It wasn't as easy as I make it sound, of course, and I once saw a grown gringo rookie bend the 3/4" steel tiller when he unexpectedly hit a shear cross current.

One of the great advantages of a pecky-pecky is that when you're traveling with a group of visitors you don't have to think of intelligent things to say because no one can hear anything except the engine, even if the muffler is good which it usually isn't. You don't even have to answer questions.

"What's the name of the bird up there in

that tree?" a visitor shouts, as if you have some sort of telescopic eyes that can identify a brown speck half a kilometer away.

"Huh?" you roar above the hammering of the engine.

"What's the name of the bird up there in that tree?"

"Huh?" you answer again, cupping your hand to your ear and hoping the bird will be out of sight by the time the visitor passes you a note.

You can carry on conversations like that for hours, just saying "huh," because mufflers are the first things to rust out on a pecky.

Another advantage is you never have to worry about falling asleep and missing any of the fascinating jungle flora and fauna, not that there's any fauna left by the time the pecky roars past. The whole boat vibrates so much that if you lay your head down your nose and eyeballs start to itch and your cheeks shake and you can feel your brain slowly dissolving into mush.

Of course there's also the benefit that no one in a pecky-pecky will ever sneak up on you.

"I wonder who's coming," the Indians would suddenly say. Machis have an uncanny ability to hear things that white people never will and they could tell us two days in advance that a pecky-pecky was coming up the river. That gave plenty of time to build an extra room on the house, hunt for some fresh meat or clean up the school before the guests arrived.

Relatively speaking, peckies were cheap to buy, cheap to operate and easy to fix. Bringing them to the jungle was like turning loose a couple pairs of rabbits — within a few years they were popping up everywhere. They became water taxis on Lake Yarinacocha, pecky-pecky-peckying their way around the lake at all hours of the day or night. In fact, they were sort of like the cicadas — one of those homey jungle sounds that you eventually can't sleep without. If the cicadas and the peckies got quiet, you could count on a good storm coming down the lake.

Out in Machi country, villagers could finally get together for soccer matches, fiestas, conferences and other special events without having to paddle and pole for a week. They could go farther to get leaves and faster to get medical help. Peckies turned their rivers into highways and interstates. For the first time in their history, they were connected. Goods and services and people and... unfortunately... epidemic germs could travel far more easily from place to place.

The best thing about putting a Briggs and Stratton on a boat was that you didn't have to modify the basic engine at all. All you did was bolt on the steering bar and the tail and the U-shaped cradle with the pin. That meant that when you got where you were going you still had an engine you could use for other things and Dad's specialty as a community development expert was in helping the Machis do more than one thing with one thing. Like using a boat engine for a lawnmower.

In the early years we mostly got to and from villages in float planes but they were slow and expensive compared to land planes, and in some places the rivers were too shallow for floats. For reasons we never understood as kids, pilots didn't like slaloming around the rocks while they gained speed. Anyway, we started building more and more airstrips, some of which weren't much of an improvement over just dodging around rocks in the river.

The trick was in keeping the grass on the airstrips cut. You could walk for three years through the jungle and never see a blade of grass, but as soon as you made an airstrip the grass would take over. You'd think there was a bunch of grass seed out there in space just waiting for a place to land. That probably has more to do with global warming than we think — all the grass seed landing on our airstrips left holes in the ozone. You may think that's a ridiculous notion, but the Machis would believe it if I could just find the right way to say it. They don't have a word for ozone.

Anyway, it took a small army of Machis with machetes to cut the grass on an airstrip that was 300 yards long and 20 yards wide, so Dad and a mechanically inclined friend from the mountains figured out a way to make a lawn mower out of a pecky engine. After 2 years of ignoring laughing skeptics and experimenting with several failed versions that were pretty ridiculous, they eventually got the engine properly mounted on a sturdy steel frame with big metal wheels in the back and little wheels in the front and a huge mower blade underneath, made from a truck spring. Two twisted belts hooked the vertical drive shaft pulley to the horizontal blade shaft pulley and if you had a Tarzan available to push the monstrosity he could cut an airstrip in 2 hours using one gallon of gas. The whole thing was bolted together instead of welded, so that anyone with a strong grip and callused fingers could fix it.

The final version impressed everyone. It could cut weeds a yard high and never wore out and if you wonder why you've never seen one it's only because they weighed more than you and your wife put together and had a turning radius of about fifteen feet and it would take your whole family to push it. For airstrips that was fine but neither you nor your neighbors would want it in your backyard.

Then there were the sawmills. As you might guess, in the jungle there are a *lot* of trees. The problem is that making boards out of trees with an ax and a machete is a bit tedious and wastes a lot of wood and the result is boards that look a little too much like the sides of canoes. The Machis made their first school benches and tables like that, and I can't say they were very comfortable to sit or write on.

There were huge sawmills in Pucallpa and lots of people who were eager to take the Machiguenga's best trees down there to sell for a handsome profit. None of that did the Machis any good, of course, since they didn't get much of the money and it wasn't practical to haul the boards back upriver.

Pecky engines changed all of that. With just two world class weightlifters you could hoist the engine off a boat or lawnmower frame and hook it up to a driveshaft with a huge sawblade attached to it. Then, by rigging up a carriage on steel wheels you could run a small log through the blade, churning out gloriously flat lumber by the meter.

Mind you, even a nine-horse Briggs and Stratton isn't the most powerful thing on earth, though the Machis thought so. It took a lot of patience to push a log through without bogging the engine down, but compared to making planks with a machete it was a quantum leap forward and sort of in the same ballpark as the creation of the world — "Let there be boards. And there were boards. And they were good boards."

Church pews became bearable, school benches didn't put bunions on buns, desks actually held books, boards replaced palm slats in a few progressive houses. We, of course, thought to ourselves that the progress made villages a little less quaint, but then the Machis weren't all that interested in quaint. Did we use machetes and axes to make our school benches at Yarinacocha? Well… no.

I said up above that pecky engines were workhorses that lasted forever. Not quite. Sooner than anyone wished, they began to wear out, break down, fall in the drink, or otherwise quit peckying. Rather than count it a blessing and let them rot in welcome silence, different groups began to offer classes in small engine repair.

You can imagine the challenge of teaching basic engine repair to Indians whose most complex tool is a bow and arrow. Dad's first class started with an engine block, pliers, screw driver and one wrench. Not even any duct tape or baling wire. Dad taught one student from the mountains and then that student began teaching Indians from around the jungle. Once he finally got a whole engine to work with, he would take a bunch of students out in the lake and kill the engine by flooding it, starving it or shorting it and the students had to get it running again. The amazing thing is that the engine ever ran long enough that the teacher had to purposely stop it.

The Indians caught on quickly and became geniuses at keeping the engines running, carving their own bushings out of hardwoods and making gaskets out of tin foil and devising throttle controls that only they could work in the middle of a foaming rapid. Some could pretty nearly rebuild a whole engine with a pair of pliers, a screw driver and a jack knife.

Those engine repair classes at Yarinacocha were a godsend for Terry and me. Every once in a while someone out in a village would send an engine to our linguistic center to be worked on, and blessing of blessings, it had to sit at our house in Yarinacocha for weeks or months waiting to go back out to the village. Terry and I and our mechanically inclined friends thought our ministry to the Indians could be to run the engines now and then so they didn't just rust.

Now you have to understand that one of

the best gifts our dad ever gave us was fifteen barrels of junk. He'd gotten word that the maintenance shop at the linguistic center was about to throw a whole slew of odds and ends into a landfill to get it out of the way.

"Why don't you just bring it over to our house?" Dad asked. "The boys will have fun with it." I think he considered himself one of the boys.

We couldn't have been happier if we'd just been given a gift certificate to a hardware store. That pile of rusting junk was full of goodies and riches that kept us inventing for four years. Can you imagine getting your very own Maytag wringer washing machine gear box, complete with a lever for forward and reverse? By the time we'd attached that to an old go-cart frame and an electric motor we could speed along at a breathtaking five miles per hour, going forward until the extension cord ran out and then backward until it ran out the other direction.

When we got tired of the extension cord limitations, we hooked the gear box up to an old pair of bike peddles and made a paddle wheel canoe that could actually back away from the bank. None of our contraptions lasted very long or worked particularly well but the possibilities were endless.

With the coming of pecky engines,

go-carts took on a whole new flavor. Now we didn't need extension cords. Now we could go more than five miles an hour. Now we could kill ourselves with very little effort.

The best go-cart I remember used a red frame that Terry got from someone who had left to go back to the USA. The frame wasn't really made for that big an engine. Actually, nothing but cars are made for that big of an engine, so it took a little work to get the pecky perched where it wouldn't break the frame or tip the go-cart over.

There were several versions of that go-cart, and I don't even remember exactly who put together the one Towner and I took out for a test run one dusty, hot afternoon. As usual, our junk pile wasn't quite complete so we had to either patch together the controls or just do without them. On this particular cart, there was no throttle control and no brakes. Once your pit crew had started the engine, you just hung on for dear life until someone stopped the engine, which wasn't as easy as it sounds.

Although the engine had just been repaired, it was running a little spasmodically, sometimes sputtering and then suddenly charging full ahead. What with the weight problem and the fact that the engine was on the back and was massively overpowered, every surge inevitably resulted in a wheelie, which was pretty exhilarating.

We dragged the cart out to the road behind our house — a road that led down past neighbors' houses and eventually past the finance office where Towner's mom worked. It was a bad choice of location, what with the nice picket fence just across the road from the finance office.

"You go first," said Towner. That was a bad sign.

"No, you're better at this stuff. You go first," I answered quite generously.

We insisted back and forth and Towner eventually climbed on first. He had every bit as much courage as the early astronauts who strapped themselves to a Saturn 5 rocket and headed for outer space.

My job was to both start and stop the cart. I'd start it the time honored way, pulling on a starter rope that I wrapped around a little pulley on the crankshaft. Once it started, I'd run alongside until it was time to stop, then reach down and press a thin strip of metal against the spark plug. We used to have the driver do that, but it was a little too hard to reach back and find that metal strip while he was steering over bumpy roads, and if he missed the metal strip and touched the spark plug he'd feel like he'd just been hit by a bolt of lightning. Not many of us were ready for that much excitement all at once.

I pulled a couple of times, and the engine pounded to life. The front wheels came right off the ground, which was thrilling except that Towner couldn't steer. Off he went, faster than we'd imagined in a direction that the cart chose all by itself.

"Kill the engine," he shouted, leaving me in the dust. I raced like the wind, in vain. Even if I could catch up, I wasn't about to poke my fingers around the spark plug while the cart was bouncing and I was running.

For a moment there was a sputter. We were already past Goodall's old house by now, and the front wheels touched down in time for Towner to get the cart straightened. I started to catch up, but then with a great roar he was off again, launched into a complete lack of control. Past the print shop he raced before another sputter got him back in the right direction. Before I could get close enough to kill the engine he wheelied yet again, hung on like a barnacle while the go-cart veered left, and smashed into the fence, splintering pickets.

The engine died all by itself, I'm thankful to say, and when Towner's mother came out of the office to see what the commotion was, he was happily quite unharmed. I don't even think we got punished considering it was the engine's fault, but it did show poor judgment on our part, and we knew it. We never should have tried it out so close to where his mom worked. The next time we tried it we were more cautious — we took it to the lake road where there weren't so many buildings. That time when the wheels left the ground and the engine finally died, I was precariously close to the edge of a fifty-foot dropoff, but at least my mother wasn't there to witness it.

If we'd been able to solve the go-carts' steering and braking problems, we could have introduced something a lot more fun than boats, lawnmowers and sawmills to the Machiguengas. But then they already had enough life-threatening things to deal with and didn't need one more way to die, no matter how much fun it might be.

# Chapter 9

## *The Landslide*

"Tell you what," Uncle Jim announced in January of 1968. "I've got a special reward for you." That should have been warning enough, but we kept listening anyway. "I'll take any of you who've gotten your Trailblazer rank by March on a week-long camping trip into the mountains. We'll go see the ruins at Huanuco Viejo."

I'm not sure why any of us in our Boy's Brigade club thought a camping trip in the mountains in an ancient Ford pickup truck during rainy season would be a reward and none of us was particularly interested in the ruins at Huanuco Viejo. I'm not even sure what Uncle Jim's motivation was, since he knew better than most that every trip we ever went on turned into a disaster. Still, he thought the very worst kind of disaster was sitting all day in meetings and I suspect that he planned it all so he could skip a week long conference that he knew he'd be required to attend.

Our club was the Yarinacocha chapter of the Christian Service Brigade, designed similarly to the Boy Scouts, with various ranks and merit badges that you could earn if you were ambitious. If you weren't all that ambitious you attended the meetings once a week, got cut and scratched and bug bit playing capture the flag in the waist-high grass at night, and that was that. We never went in that grass in the daytime — we didn't want to see what all might be living in it.

Apart from the fact that we lived in the jungle, what made our club different from other similar clubs was that Uncle Jim was our leader. Since Uncle Jim could do absolutely anything he put his mind to, he didn't think the standard manuals and texts ever demanded enough of us when it came to getting merit badges.

When I decided to get my bicycling badge, for example, the text required me to learn how a derailleur worked and go for a bit of a ride.

Uncle Jim thought I ought to know how to make a derailleur out of old sewing machine parts and ride my bike 500 miles over the Andes to Lima.

We settled for an 120-mile overnight to a little town called Tournavista. My friend Andy and I ended up carrying our bicycles for ten kilometers in a pouring rain on a sticky clay road that completely disabled the derraileurs, the brakes, the wheels and us. Even then the badge was in question.

"Maybe you should get the backpacking badge instead" Uncle Jim mused without a hint of humor, "since you didn't really ride the whole way." Real funny.

Anyway, one of the higher ranks some of us pursued was appropriately called Trailblazer and we worked valiantly for Uncle Jim's special reward. Seven of us ended up in the pickup just after lunch on a Saturday afternoon. Two of the luckiest sat in the front with Uncle Jim and the rest sat on the tailgate or huddled under a homemade plywood cap that covered about half of the bed. It was supposed to keep things dry but usually just kept the sun from drying out things that had gotten wet. We shouted and laughed and waved goodbye to people along the way.

There's a lot that could be said about the road from Yarinacocha to the mountains, but I'll skip it. Relatively speaking it was quite comfortable even though we were rattled, banged, covered with dust, sprinkled with rain and sore and smelly from sitting on surplus ammunition boxes and mushy bananas respectively. That was the good part. When the bananas got irretrievably mushy, we hurled them at roadside cows and... uhh... well... sometimes there were people by the cows.

In those days Peru was fabulously free of terrorists and drug thugs and the check points we passed were mainly used to control traffic on the one-way roads. Since construction and repairs were being done in the mountains, many sections of the road were reduced to one-lane mudholes. Heavy trucks and buses groaned their way into the mountains on "up" days; others creaked back toward the jungle on "down" days.

Our first night we slept in a gorgeous canyon under a cloudless sky, listening to the river as it crashed over boulders and into craggy banks. Since we only had one huge military surplus tent, and since it was full of rat holes and torn seams, cloudless skies were a gift from God himself. The tent was definitely a last resort, and we'd sleep under rocks, trucks, bridges, ferns or pot lids to keep from having to put it up. It was easy to imagine a whole platoon of soldiers dying as they fought with their tent.

In the morning we flung sleeping gear into the back of the truck, swallowed whole lumps of Quaker Oats that we'd been too lazy to stir, washed our dishes in cold brown river water and took off again on a long slow climb, banging and bouncing on the high ridge of mud and rocks that formed between the two ruts. Since the ruts were made by heavy trucks with higher clearances, our tie rod, oil pan, rear axle, spare tire and bumpers all sort of sledded us along.

Every once in a while all four wheels were on the ground at the same time, but that was pretty rare. Regular stops for tightening and straightening gave us welcome opportunities to climb trees for fruit, heave rocks into the river far below, sail giant fern leaves like gliders or just hurl mud balls at each other.

Our scenic drive rattled us up to a cool muddy summit flanked by tea gardens. Then we bounced and dragged down into the tiny town of Tingo Maria where we gulped a mountain of mediocre Chinese fried rice while Uncle Jim tightened and straightened. He loved working on old cars, and this one was aging nicely before our very eyes.

After lunch it was up again through a stunning narrow valley with orchids lining one side of the road. We took turns swinging Lloyd's net from the back of the pickup at

passing butterflies. It's a bad sign when
butterflies are going faster than you are.
Lloyd was one of those weird kids who knew
the scientific names of everything we swung
at, whereas the rest of us pretty much boiled
life down to two species: edible and
non-edible. Butterflies were the latter,
unless you were really hungry.

Anyway Lloyd had quite a collection,
though the ones we caught from the back of
the pickup weren't exactly gorgeous by the
time he got them home. Butterflies aren't
all that exciting without wings, even if you
do know their scientific name. Of course
kids like Lloyd could probably come up with
the scientific name for a detached thorax.
Or whatever that non-edible thing is that
explodes when it hits the windshield.

About 4:45 we arrived at yet another
major construction zone just as a blasting
rain started, kind of like God was mixing
the wet ingredients with the dry
ingredients and the construction workers
were stirring. We fishtailed and skidded up
the mountain, narrowly avoiding the sheer
cliff on one side and the deep ditch on the
other. At one point a construction worker
stopped us to hitch a ride home from his
drunken weekend in Tingo Maria. Uncle
Jim told him we were already overloaded,
but he jumped on the running board
anyway and stuck tight as a leech while we

swayed and lurched. From the smell of his breath, he'd already been swaying and lurching for some time.

After a miserable blue-lipped hour the pickup slid to a complete stop. We in the back poked our heads out to see a little Opel sedan stuck right in the middle of the road.

"Just go around it," our barnacle on the running board shouted, waving his free arm. "You don't need to stop." Now that he had a ride, he didn't particularly care about anyone else's troubles and he shouted obnoxiously enough that Uncle Jim did what he said. We got too close to the ditch. Lost all our traction. Slid roaring and spinning into the slush, rear wheels flinging mud uselessly.

All seven of us automatically leaped out to push, kind of like you'd jump to catch a baby falling off a ladder. We grunted like pigs and strained like oxen and everyone yelled orders that left us all pushing in different directions at the same time. Not that it mattered. The truck sank up to the running boards in soupy mud as if it was just sort of ready for a rest.

"What's that smell?" asked Peach. It was kind of a hot burning smell, but it was hard to tell if it was us, muddy water on the engine, or our food supply. We gave up and went over to help push the Opel out.

By the time we had raised the Opel to

higher ground, the pickup was drowning. The whole road was a stream of thick muddy water. Small landslides dumped more mud into the ditch. Everyone from the Opel, grateful for our help, joined us to push on the pickup again. Uncle Jim tried digging with a little shovel, which was sort of like trying to stop an avalanche with a spoon. We shoved frantically, the engine roared as if it was ready to blow and... hmmm... funny thing... the wheels weren't turning.

"The clutch is burned out," Uncle Jim muttered wearily as he slumped out into knee deep slop. I wondered if he was thinking that the conference wouldn't have been so bad after all.

At least now we knew what smelled so bad and it wasn't our food supply. We might be buried by morning, but we would have food and transportation with us for the afterlife. The Incas who once roamed these mountains would have been proud.

In between bursts of digging, pushing, and discussing our options, as if we had any, we watched our first massive landslide, which would have been a lot more fun if it had been a bit farther away. With a ferocious roar, mud, boulders and plants crashed onto the road, shook it apart and carried a huge chunk of it down the mountain in front of us.

"Wow!" we all breathed collectively, glad to still be breathing. Unfortunately, since that was the only road to the Inca ruins, our spirits crashed into the river with the debris. We knew our special treat was over, whether or not we could ever get out of the ditch.

An early darkness soon obliterated our view of everything except mud. We tried various ways to keep plastic tied over our stuff, which was already soaked, but mostly we stood around shivering and watching the rain come down. One would have thought that kids raised in the rain forest would have brought rain gear, but no, we hadn't thought of it. Uncle Jim, who could fix almost anything, quit digging and worked on the clutch, figuring if he could adjust it a little there might still be some life in it. He didn't look quite so excited to be working on his old car now that he had to float on his back in the mud to get under it.

Around 8:00 we heard the high pitched whine of a motorcycle coming up the road. It was a university student who said he absolutely had to get to the next town so he could get some papers signed. We told him there wasn't any road left up ahead but he slithered on past us, soaking wet and caked with mud, and barged headlong into the rubble left from the landslide. *Cool*, we thought, *what a guy*! Suddenly there was a loud clattery sound like there were rocks in his cylinder. *Not cool*, we thought, *what an idiot*! Not that we wouldn't have done the same thing, given the chance.

Eventually the mudman driver materialized out of the darkness pushing his motorcycle. He guessed he didn't absolutely have to get the papers signed after all and he was grateful to have such fascinating company while we waited together.

Exhausted from our day's fun, we began to settle in for the night, huddled together like refugees under wet blankets in the back of the pickup. Lloyd, who could immediately fall asleep anywhere, was already unconscious and the rest of us close to it when we heard something clanking and splashing down the mountain.

"What's that?" Andy mumbled as if any of us would know. We untangled arms and legs until we were pretty sure we each had our own and kind of fell out of the pickup trying to hobble on numb legs that were still asleep. A giant Caterpillar bulldozer was coming to our rescue and since it was definitely more fun to watch a bulldozer at work than to try and doze ourselves, we stared through bleary red eyes.

With its headlight blasting away the soggy darkness, the tractor pushed and shoved and bullied aside the biggest boulders, sending them cascading into the black void. As soon as the driver could get through he did, leaving behind what might generously be considered a road. Just as quickly, he went right past us, not stopping to pull us out. It was like witnessing the Second Coming and realizing that you've been left behind. He rattled away and we watched forlornly as his headlights swept the sides of the mountains before finally disappearing around a bend.

When that hope turned to a nope, we decided once again to try and get out of the ditch on our own, though I'm not exactly sure why we thought we'd have any more luck this time than we did with more people and less mud last time. We dug a little more, started the engine, and strained like a team of Clydesdales, mostly all pushing in the same direction at the same time.

Forward, reverse, forward, reverse, forward, reverse. The engine roared and the wheels splattered us with mud and the clutch sizzled and stank and our bare feet bled from the sharp rocks. At first there was nothing, then an inch each way, then a foot. We yelled at each other, yelled at the car, yelled at life in general and the Caterpillar driver in particular. Adrenaline flooding us, we heaved for all we were worth one way, then dove out of the way when Uncle Jim reversed directions, since he would happily have used our bodies for extra traction about then.

So, yelling and pushing and scrambling, we rocked back and forth until suddenly the truck hit a bit of solid ground and clambered out of the ditch. Cheering, we helped it through a tight U-turn, yelled thanks and good-bye to the cyclist and leaped in before Uncle Jim could leave us behind. The last we saw of the cyclist, he was snuggled up to his motorcycle waiting for someone with more room than we had.

We raced down the slippery one-lane road in wild retreat at a heart stopping ten to fifteen miles per hour, the soggy mountains sliding down around us. Those of us in the back of the old pickup were thrown blindly from side to side, desperately trying to hang on to the truck and our luggage. Whenever we felt the truck slowing down too much we instantly leaped out to push, then raced to get back in, since Uncle Jim never stopped to count heads. The deteriorating clutch got worse with each slowdown, but for over an hour we kept moving.

About the time we thought we might actually survive this nightmare, we came to a soft but definite stop, and jumped out into a sea of mud. Unsuspecting, Uncle Jim had driven into a soupy lake and the momentum had carried us too far too fast. The clutch had died. Rocks rained on us, making soft "schplots" in the muddy lake and bouncing loudly on the hood of the pickup. If Uncle Jim was scared, he did a good job of hiding it. The rest of us weren't so noble.

Barefoot, Andy and I waded and then hobbled back up the road to where a truck had stopped, learning from our experience.

"Do you have a cable?" we asked breathlessly. "If we don't get out we'll get killed."

"Si," he answered. "I have a cable, but I can't get close enough to reach you."

Shivering uncontrollably, we slogged back to the pickup, arriving just in time to hear the truck driver yelling for one of us to come back. This time Terry sloshed toward him to hear the good news that there was an equipment depot back around the corner and we might be able to get a Caterpillar to pull us out. Terry disappeared into the dark with the truck driver's helper and the rest of us waited without much hope, up to our knees in slush.

Incredibly, when Terry came back he was riding in a Caterpillar D8 with a sleepy driver. Thank God! The Cat had no cable, but the driver boldly barged right into the mess and pushed us out, surfing us along on a wave of mud. He washed us up onto a solid area, said we were welcome and went back to bed.

We wished fervently that we could go back to bed. With Uncle Jim relatively stretched out in the cab, the rest of us crowded into the back of the narrow pickup. The blankets were wet, everything was muddy, there were still ammo boxes and a fifteen gallon barrel in the way, rain soaked anything that stuck out from under the plywood hood and none of us wanted to touch each other. Lloyd was asleep in seconds. The rest of us squirmed and scrunched and eventually got out to talk to passengers and drivers of the trucks and buses that were lining up behind us, all waiting for the road to be repaired.

At some point in the eternal night I dug out a little tarp, wrapped my wet blanket around me and fell asleep under a truck, only waking up when rocks fell too close, and only going back into the pickup when my chattering teeth drove me to it. As special rewards went, this one was definitely turning into one of the worst.

# Chapter 10

## *The Ruins*

At 4:30 in the morning a grunting bulldozer gave us an excuse to get up. It was such hard work trying to sleep that we really needed a rest anyway. The dozer was rebuilding the road right behind us so that it could get far enough to remake the road right in front of us.

We all tumbled out of the pickup to watch, wincing on sore feet and trying to get frozen legs and arms to flex. We could have used a physical therapist. Just as the sun came up the dozer cloppety-clopped past and started on the lake of mud that had sunk us. For another hour and a half tidal waves of slush and rock rolled over the cliff until there was enough of a road to try moving some of the cars, buses, motorcycles and trucks that had lined up behind us.

The luckiest part of the whole trip, apart from living through the night before, was that we were first in line and we were stuck dead in the middle of the narrow road. One of the earliest lessons of our lives was that you should never, never break down or get stuck where other vehicles can just go around you. We couldn't go anywhere, what with our burned out clutch, but neither could anyone else.

Uncle Jim started the engine and raced it a few times to impress everyone. We pushed briefly, the car rolled back into the mud hole and that was that. Just like the night before. Unlike the night before, however, we now had about a dozen impatient drivers, a couple hundred cranky bus passengers and a smattering of busy construction workers who all wanted us through the mess so that they could be on their way. We flashed huge smiles that cracked the dried mud on our faces, shrugged our sunburned shoulders and did a bangup job of looking helpless while air horns blasted and people yelled.

Eventually, out of frustration or a genuine desire to be helpful, the bulldozer driver moved up behind us and shoved us through, looking a bit like a tattered piece of driftwood being bullied by a tugboat. Once past the deepest mud, the caterpillar abandoned us, but some desperate men helped push us on down the road to a wider spot, where a strategically placed tractor could shove us off the road. We were especially happy to see that one of the pushers was the university student we'd left hugging his motorcycle the night before, still without his urgent papers.

Finally cast aside, out of everyone's way, we settled down to shredded wheat and banana bread while a parade of filthy vehicles roared past, splattering us. Uncle Jim walked to a stream a half mile away to get washed up in preparation for climbing under the truck and taking out the clutch. I don't remember why he washed up before squirming into the mud, but there must have been a good reason.

Since the clutch plates fell out in charred bits and pieces, it was crystal clear even to those of us without our mechanic's merit badges that we needed parts and it didn't take a Trailblazer to know that there weren't any parts stores around the corner.

By the time we collectively figured this out, the vehicles that had been trapped behind us were all in front of us and the road had been closed to further traffic. Our only chances to hitch a ride were gone. Suddenly, the fifty miles between us and Tingo Maria seemed a very long walk.

Shortly after we'd cleaned up the breakfast dishes, Uncle Jim and I started hiking. I don't remember why I went along. It's true that I loved doing things with Uncle Jim, and it's true that I'd rather be walking than sitting around, but it still seems really stupid of me. Uncle Jim was a hiker who loved to get out and go. I was a high schooler who just loved to get there, preferably on wheels. He walked strong and steady and didn't care if he ate anything all day. I tried to keep up and thought about food the whole way.

Barefoot, the sharp rocks slashed and gashed. In shoes, my feet blistered. I alternated so that at least the sores would be evenly spread.

Around noon we caught up with four truckers who had stopped for a long lunch and a few beers at a clapboard kitchen. Uncle Jim didn't even ask for a ride.

"I've sort of got in the habit of walking," he said.

"Me too," I answered bravely, nodding and smiling and lying through my teeth.

Fortunately, the truckers came by before I died, and this time we climbed aboard. "You've walked about 25 miles," they said. "That was far enough," I said. "We could have made it by supper time," Uncle Jim said.

It only took a couple of hours to get the rest of the way to Tingo and get new parts. We didn't take time to eat because Uncle Jim didn't think it was all that important and figured we could walk all night for fifty more miles on a chocolate bar apiece. Who was I to argue?

I really believe God saw what Uncle Jim didn't — my imminent death — and sent angels to take charge. We immediately caught a succession of rides in construction pickups and Jeeps that delivered us right to our broken down pickup just as the sun set.

The rest of the guys had already spread their bedding beside the road, so I whipped up some cheese sandwiches while they packed up and Uncle Jim put the clutch back together. In a few quick minutes we'd head back to Tingo for the night and then on home in the morning. We'd already had enough of a treat for one trip.

The sunset was stunning. A fingernail moon sparkled just above the mountains.

"It almost makes me regret turning back," Uncle Jim said wistfully. He was probably thinking that he'd have to sit through the conference after all.

We went through all the motions of preparing for a hasty departure, some eagerly and some of us feeling like mud wrestlers who'd just lost a major fight. Uncle Jim once again walked to the stream to wash up and we waited, talking softly.

It was about then that a VW bug skittered past us, chased by a Chevy sedan that looked as if it might be trying to eat the bug. Both were weaving and dodging and bouncing, but they were going more or less steadily in the direction we had wanted to go. Just after they passed, a truck came down the mountain, so we stopped it and asked the driver how the road to Huanuco was.

"Bien feo," he answered, sounding like "really ugly" was the best thing he could say for it. "It's impossible to get through in a little pickup like that."

"What about that VW?" I asked searching for something more encouraging.

"He's stupid."

When Uncle Jim got back, he sat in the cab finally eating his sandwiches while Andy and Terry and I talked to him.

"That truck driver that just came by said the road's really ugly," I quoted.

"Yeah," he sighed.

"Did you see those two cars come past?" we wondered.

"No."

"A VW bug and a little Chevy headed for Huanuco."

"A Beetle?" he asked raising one eyebrow

and our hopes. "Going to Huanuco?" We nodded.

"Well, if they think they can make it, I suppose we can."

Terry and Andy and I nodded enthusiastically, not mentioning that the truck driver had used the word 'estupido.' Nor did any of us mention the obvious — that you don't do something stupid just because other people are stupid.

We knew the younger guys were ready to go home, having already had about as much fun as they could stand, so we didn't ask them what they thought. Everyone got in, Uncle Jim turned the truck around and we roared back up the mountain, the wheels thankfully turning now when the engine did.

We strained to see in the total blackness, and tried to stave off rigor mortis with thin wind breakers. Like the night before, we skidded and swayed and hung on for dear life. We'd been going for about an hour when we caught up with the VW and the Chevy. The Chevy was stuck right in the middle of the road with transmission trouble so we all piled out to help.

The pathetic little car's wheels were locked up, so instead of pushing we just gathered around it, grabbed ahold of muddy parts and bounced it out of the way, lifting and dropping in a surprisingly coordinated rhythm. As we left, the Chevy's friends in the VW were retreating back to Tingo Maria for parts. I should have told them to leave the car and walk since it had been such a fun experience for me.

We kept going until past midnight. Since we were out of synch with the flow of traffic that day, we constantly had to look for places to slide off the road and let trucks squeeze past, our fenders brushing the mud off each other. We jumped out to push twice and the rest of the time huddled together for warmth. Finally exhausted, Uncle Jim pulled over to the side and we slept like the dead on scattered ground cloths under wet blankets.

The next day we finally went through Huanuco, stopping just long enough to scavenge life-saving ice cream bars and chocolate while Uncle Jim shopped for enough parts to keep the pickup from disintegrating. The back bumper dangled pathetically after doing battle with so many rocks during the night.

Now we just had to get to the ruins and our trip would be complete. We left the main highway and climbed steeply to La Union, thousands of feet above sea level, stopping occasionally to take pictures of cactuses and eucalyptus groves. Most of the vehicles we passed were practical half truck/half bus combos especially designed for the Quechua

Indians who needed to get their produce to market. The designer probably didn't foresee ten people per seat, especially stocky Quechua women wearing four or five thick skirts apiece.

We could see several faces staring at us through each window, and the back sections bulged with vegetables and animals and extra children. One truck had a particularly strange sounding horn that turned out to be a trumpet player who somehow found enough oxygen to entertain the countryside as he bounced along.

Late in the afternoon we came to a hot springs that promised our first baths this trip, except for Uncle Jim, who had bathed before he climbed under the truck that time. It seemed worth a stop and when we found that we could get a room with four beds in it plus a real dinner, we considered it a gift from God.

We immediately transferred our smelly luggage from the pickup to the hotel, changed into fermented swim suits and dived into therapeutically hot water that flowed through a nicely tiled pool. Within minutes we were providing the wide-eyed Quechuas with the greatest show on earth: pyramids, flips, tidal waves and blind man's tag. Most people, it seems, just sat around relaxing in the hot water for an hour, which seemed to us a colossal waste of such a blessing.

When our hour was up we reluctantly exited into the cold air, shivered into dry clothes and headed for the restaurant, which was a little less of a blessing than the pool. A cat sat on the cook's table eating out of one of his pots, which at least encouraged us that the food might be safe. The cat, after all, looked healthy.

The food was filling, but that's about all that could be said for it. Between efforts to keep the cat from eating it before we could, we swallowed cold chicken soup, cold rice and cold potatoes into our cold stomachs, our teeth chattering and chewing. Since it wasn't exactly the kind of place where you'd want to linger, we didn't. We were in bed by 8:00, with two to a bed except that Terry wanted to sleep on the floor, so Uncle Jim got his bed to himself.

I can't say that we woke up refreshed. The beds sagged so badly we rolled into each other all night. Plus Swaug had walked outside in his sleep, woken up in the cold and come back in completely disoriented. He tapped on legs and banged into beds and kept asking, "Is that you, Charlie?" For some reason I don't remember, Swaug always called Peach "Charlie." We called him Peach because of his fuzzy cheeks. Not that any of that mattered in the middle of the night — the point is, Swaug managed to wake everyone up before he finally found his way back under warm blankets.

At first light we boarded the pickup again for the ride to the ruins, following a horse trail off through the high grassy plains. It only took an hour of scrambling over and around boulders to get to the ruins, where we jumped out to fix pancakes under dark clouds before our exploration. Swaug danced from box to box trying to keep his bare feet off the frosty ground. It turned out he'd forgotten to bring any shoes at all on the trip. The rest of us had at least brought them, even though we didn't wear them very often.

We went to look at the Inca's handiwork while Swaug scattered our wet clothes and bedding out to dry in the hoped for sun.

"I don't really want to see the ruins anyway," he said, hopping.

Of course we'll never know what we actually saw, since the Incas didn't leave a guidebook. On the other hand, there was a shepherd near the ruins whose interpretations helped along our imaginations. According to him, there was a nice spot for the soldiers to bathe in 35-degree creek water, a nicer spot for the royalty to bathe in water that used to be channeled from the hot springs, a torture chamber with separate sections for men and women, a fortress with superb rock work, and granaries on the mountainside still in use by the Inca's descendants. *If I were an Inca's descendent,* I thought as I blew on blue fingers, *I'd figure out a way to still be using the royalty's hot tub.*

Although it wasn't the most spectacular set of ruins in Peru, it still inspired us to imagine a mighty civilization gone by, and gave us a profound respect for a group of people who valued such perfection in their workmanship, one stone at a time.

Back at the truck in the early afternoon we fixed a hot stew that never quite got done in the altitude and cut up watermelons that had been chilling in the stream nearby. Gathered our scattered clothes, loaded the truck and bounced back to the hot springs. We'd collected our Trailblazer award. Now it was just a matter of surviving until we got back home. We went back to the hot pool, but with less enthusiasm since some of us had headaches and upset stomachs. Maybe the cat was wrong after all. Or more likely the 13,000-foot altitude was taking it's toll.

It wasn't a bad night, even though I woke up to find that Dennis had thrown up on my bathing suit during the night. I'd left it drying on the railing outside our room, it had fallen into the ditch below, and Dennis didn't look before he launched. By now there wasn't a whole lot of difference between the rest of our clothes and my

barfed-on bathing suit anyway, so it didn't
matter.

Terry and Andy and I, I'm sorry to say,
acted like the bullying upper classmen we
were and packed the truck so that the three
of us could comfortably sit on soft duffels
and lean against more soft duffels under the
shade of the hood. I'm not proud of this, but
I thought I'd better put it in because some
of the other guys may read this story, and
they'll surely remember the difference
between our ride down the mountain on
duffels and theirs on boxes and cans.

There's no point in describing all the
gory details. By early evening we had
burned out the generator, pushed ourselves
out of a few more mudholes, scorched our
tonsils on hot peppers that looked like sweet
peppers floating innocently in delicious
soup, set up the Army tent across the river
from Huanuco and settled in for the night.
By now Swaug, Dennis, Terry, and Lloyd
had all vomited their day's foragings onto
the roadside scenery, so the leaky Army
tent looked more like a MASH unit than a
vacation spot. I'm not even sure why we put
it up. The only thing it did in the rain was
funnel water onto our blankets, which it
began doing around midnight.

We ran around in the darkness futiley
trying to secure the sides and moved from
spot to spot to dodge frigid waterfalls and

streams that the tent created with amazing efficiency. Somehow we could get downpours inside from sprinkles outside, which would have made the tent extremely useful in the desert. For those who finally did find dry spots, the sides of the tent flapped boisterously, shaking water like a dog that's just been swimming. All in all, I can't say it was a restful night nor even a particularly bonding experience. About 2:00 a.m., in fact, we hated each other and virtually said so.

The next day we made it all the way through Tingo Maria and back to the Boqueron. We got there at four in the morning, which sounds like it would make a good story. It would, but by now landslides, mudholes, broken car parts, bone numbing cold, semi-starvation, bruised bodies and long waits had gotten boring. The only reason we stopped was that another landslide had filled the road with another ocean of muck, but even that's not very interesting anymore. We just slept in the truck, the fumes from our baggage and bodies basically knocking us out for a couple of hours.

Rumor had it that the road was blocked at the same place we'd been pushed out by the Cat a few nights before. We decided to walk down and have a look — a walk past four kilometers of vehicles that had been waiting up to three days to get through. Minus bathroom facilities and restaurants, there was a crowd of really hungry, impatient people watching the construction equipment shove waves of mud aside and dump truckloads of rock into the bottomless pit.

At two o'clock they said we'd be through at three; at three o'clock they said five, at five they said six until we all gave up. At one point the impatient truck drivers angrily blocked the whole road so construction supervisors couldn't get through, loudly yelling that it was time to open the road. I'm not exactly sure what the supervisors were supposed to open, since there wasn't a road yet, but it was good entertainment watching the riot.

We finally gave up, hitched a ride back to our pickup and spread out for the night on whatever we could find: Andy and Lloyd and I in the back of the truck, Terry and Dennis on a tarp on the ground, Swaug and Peach in the back of an empty truck, Uncle Jim in the cab.

All the next day we waited until finally in the late afternoon we heard the glorious music of engines coming the opposite direction — a caravan of dozens of trucks and buses creaking and groaning and tearing up the road. On our side of the slide, drivers jockeyed for better positions in line, squeezing past anyone they could while we waited. Finally, at 7:30, in complete darkness, it was our turn.

You'd think people would be reasonable. You'd think they'd just let us slide along, in an orderly line, all in a row. Instead, as we approached our turn through the bottomless mudhole, one trucker in particular decided that he just had to be in front of us. In the coal black night, on a one-lane road of ruts and mud, he rode our tail until he saw a slightly wider spot in the road. Stomped on the accelerator, swerved to the left and raced alongside us, spraying us with mud and ignoring the sheer dropoff on his left. Uncle Jim didn't give an inch and we couldn't have had more fun on a wild bull, bucking and fishtailing in the dark. Still, when the wide spot began to narrow, the wildly roaring trucker just cut in on us until we had to slow down or be crushed and in the end he gained one space in the line.

The mudhole, nicely fixed in the afternoon, was shredded by now. So was the little hill on the opposite side. Two very deep ruts wound up it, flanked by walls of mud and rock that the trucks had pushed aside. Our hearts sank as we waited our turn. Truck drivers behind us asked us to please, please, please let them go first.

We waited long enough for the hill to be completely clear of vehicles, then positioned ourselved up ahead in the mud alongside the road. Uncle Jim raced the engine like a dragster at the starting line, let out the clutch and took off, shrieking the whole way in first gear. We watched him as he bounced into and out of the mudhole, throwing muck everywhere, and then head screaming for the hill, out of control as the ruts steered for him. He bounced off a big boulder that bashed in the right fender, scraped and banged on the rocks, swerved and spun and hesitated.

We were in exactly the right place at the right time. As the pickup slowed down, we lept off the mud banks to push, blasted by streams of rock shards thrown by the spinning wheels. They say you can do mighty things in an adrenaline rush. We did. The miracle was both we and the car were still running when we got to the top of the hill.

"These old pickups are hard to stop," Uncle Jim said, proudly patting the dashboard. He apparently had already forgotten that without our valiant efforts, the old pickup would have stopped long ago.

The great irony was that after we got out of all the mud, the road was bone dry, so we spent the next seven hours choking on clouds of dust stirred up by the trucks in front of us. When we got home at 2:15 in the morning, about all we could see of each other was white eyeballs and teeth. Can't think when we've ever had so much fun, and after a good bath we were all ready to go again.

# Chapter 11
## *Field Day*

It was about 6:00 in the evening and the telephone rang. Well, actually it buzzed six long times. That would be the "general" call. I picked up the heavy black handset and said "Hello, Snells are on," then listened as everyone around the center did the same thing. We were on one huge party line, so everyone could hear the day's news and announcements. People told jokes and chattered while they waited for the director to start through his list.

Although the phone system and the format changed through the years, that was

Yarinacocha — one big party line with everyone listening in. Since we only had screen windows in our houses, we didn't need telephones to keep in touch. We usually knew when the neighbors woke up, when they had a fight, and what they said to children who didn't want to go to bed. If the breeze was blowing the right direction, we even knew what they were having for lunch.

If it hadn't been for the fact that everyone was committed to the same goals, I suppose the whole place would have eventually blown apart at the seams. 250 people with 400 different opinions on how to do things is a lot to put up with on a little jungle center that you could walk across in fifteen minutes. We not only knew everyone's names, we knew everyone's dogs' names, which was quite an accomplishment in a place where there were so many dogs some people called it Purinacocha.

It didn't do to get mad at someone, since you couldn't get apart. You'd see each other at church, at the commissary, at the post office, at the swim ramp, at work, at the finance office, at school, and along the road during the day. Of course if you were madly in love with a high school girl, all the sightings were a blessing indeed.

Since we didn't have a pastor for our Sunday morning worship services, different men took turns preaching. That of course had its hazards, given that their whole audience had spent so much time with them during the week, and would again in the weeks following the sermon. I imagine it made it a bit more difficult to pick sermon topics.

For some, the close atmosphere was stifling. You couldn't do anything including burp after supper without the whole center knowing about it the next morning. Gossip traveled like grass fires in Nebraska.

On the other hand, there was never a more loving, helpful group of people to grow up with. Tiny children wandered freely and their parents knew that if they got into trouble, someone would help out. In any emergency, dozens of hands pitched in.

While sick Machis fought for their lives in our house, neighbors and colleagues took their turns, keeping watch so Dad and Mom could sleep. When someone died, everyone dropped everything to gather at our little cemetery and offer comfort and encouragement. When families left for furlough, crowds of friends gathered to see them off and then to welcome them back at the end of a long year.

Individual efforts became community projects. Everyone on the center knew that Harriet Fields and Hattie Kneeland, two single women, were trying to contact the Matses Indians. The Matses, unlike the

Machis, only wanted contact on their terms, which meant that they went on raiding parties to kill men and kidnap women and children. They had caused so much trouble for outsiders that the military was hoping to pacify them somehow, and hoped that Harriet and Hattie could help. Harriet and Hattie lived in a little hut for weeks at a time in the middle of nowhere hoping for a peaceful contact. For five years we all prayed for them as they dropped gifts along trails, talked to the people through a loudspeaker mounted on the wing of an airplane, and learned the Matses language from escapees who had risked their lives to get away from their harsh captors.

Everyone at the center also followed the contact of the wild Machis along the Mantaro River. In 1967 a withered but powerful old shaman began hearing reports about what was happening in Kompi and sent a pair of scouts to investigate. After walking three days over steep mountains to get there, the scouts looked around, got some fish hooks and left. Though they were scared to death, their reports were encouraging and the shaman decided he wanted a village in Mantaro just like the one in Kompi. He sent more scouts to ask questions and maintain contact.

In the meantime Venturo, a physically frail school teacher and pastor, had decided to reach out to the Mantaro people, among whom he had blood relatives. He landed in a small plane at Kompi, then disappeared into the rugged, sawtooth mountains. Back at Yarinacocha we all prayed and wondered if he would make it.

Three months later, news filtered out that Venturo was still alive. With the shaman's encouragement, the Machis had welcomed him enthusiastically, had formed a village of 130 people and had started to build an airstrip so that something they had never seen could fly in with people and goods they had never imagined.

Harold Davis, a partner in the Machi work, hiked in to help finish the airstrip, but although the Machis were eager, progress was slow. First an epidemic of flu blew in, leading to widespread pneumonia and seven deaths. No sooner had that passed than a powerful landowner downriver sent men with guns to force the people to move closer to him where they could work his plantations. Harold and Venturo held them off, but many terrified Machis disappeared into the jungle, returning later to find their possessions destroyed and their houses ransacked.

"We'll be back," threatened the gunmen as they left, "as soon as the white man leaves."

The old shaman, tears in his ancient

eyes, begged Harold not to abandon them.

"They've done this to us for a long, long time," he said, and told stories of previous raids when friends and family had been kidnapped or killed. "You are our only hope."

Desperation drove the people as they rolled huge boulders and enormous logs off the airstrip. Children carried off white rocks to the new school, where they used bits of charcoal to write math problems on them.

Finally in October the first little airplane swerved around one last remaining boulder and landed in Mantaro. Harold flew out to rejoin his family in Kompiroshiato and Venturo was on his own, teaching the children in school, teaching the adults out of school, dispensing medicine, counseling, trying to keep the community together.

One Sunday morning Venturo's energy and faith hit an all time low. He coughed endlessly with tuberculosis and his family had put up with months of loneliness and threats. Ready to quit, he turned to his Machiguenga Scriptures and began to read.

"As I read God's promises," he said later, "I remembered that people at Yarinacocha and all over the world were praying for me and I knew that because of their prayers, the promises would come true. A river of joy flowed into me and strengthened me."

A few months later Dad and a Swiss colleague flew into Mantaro to find dozens of Machis eager to hear more about God. They met day and night and nearly a hundred, including the old shaman, said they wanted Jesus to be their Savior and Headman. Venturo baptized many of them in a freezing river so swift that they had to hold onto each other.

When Dad returned from Mantaro and reported the news at our Sunday evening meeting, everyone on the center felt as if they had personally had a part in keeping Venturo going.

Once a year everyone got together for a conference to hear reports, plan strategies, elect administrative officers and argue like family over rules for dogs and bathing suit styles and Sunday afternoon siesta hours. The kids got to provide refreshments for coffee breaks; Towner and I made our first fortunes selling glazed donuts by the dozen.

There were several other events a year to draw us all together, including the Easter sunrise service where Mrs. Schellenberger's dog howled every time she hit a high note. Nothing else was quite so all-encompassing, however, as the annual school field day.

Field Day included events you've never heard of, and other events you've heard of but wouldn't recognize. For starts, the whole school, kindergarten through high school, was divided into two teams. Each team chose a captain and a name and a group of cheer leaders that spent weeks inventing and practicing choreographed cheers that seemed really fancy at the time, not that any of us could do splits or straight cartwheels or back flips. Seamstresses stressed their seams churning out matching outfits for anyone who wanted to match. Mascots were selected and exalted. Sawdust pits were filled, high jump bars repaired, lines marked on playing fields, refreshment crews designated. All things considered, it was grander than the Olympics, an event not to miss, and all free.

A couple months before Field Day all of the students signed up for the events they particularly wanted. Some kids, of course, didn't particularly want to participate in anything, but abstinence wasn't allowed because in a school that small everyone had to participate or there wouldn't be any competition.

For several weeks PE mostly consisted of preparing us for Field Day. Nowadays I suppose we'd say that you should practice for several years if you're going to race as a swimmer, but back then it seemed good enough that most of us just went swimming every day, jumping out of trees and playing tag under the raft. Bruce Kindberg, always a champion long distance runner, got his practice mowing lawns. Slow bike racers practiced by trying to go nowhere for as long as possible before putting their feet down. Kids entered in the board balance race walked back and forth to school with books on their heads, their eyeballs rolled upward and their tongues sticking out in concentration.

The big day always started off with a rousing meeting filled with a spirit of competitiveness and good cheer. Or several bad cheers, depending on how well the squad had done in their choreography.

"We can drown you with our *hands tied*," one captain would shout, forgetting that the first event was the tug of war and having the teams' hands tied would be a serious disadvantage. Nevertheless, everyone on his team would loyally rise and shout "Yeah, with our *hands tied*!" Mass hysteria.

"Can we *beat* them?" the other captain would shout back, and every voice from the squeakiest to the deepest would shout "*Beat* em? We can *bury* em." Fortunately parents had to remain neutral, since there was a conscious attempt to divide the kids in any one family between the two teams. That kept the linguistic center from deteriorating into a war zone during field days.

"The goal," we were always solemnly

reminded, "is not so much to win but to be a good sport, win or lose." Yeah right. We'd all seen our teachers and parents playing volleyball and basketball and knew that whatever they might say in the auditorium, winning was what it was all about.

I'm not sure why the tug-of-war was always the first event. Maybe it was so that everyone started off with similar disadvantages, like rope-burned hands, toes smashed by overly zealous team mates, aching arms and wobbly legs. Those tug-of-wars defined the day and put to rest any notion that sportsmanship was better than winning. Captains yelled, parents yelled, teachers yelled, participants yelled as they dug their bare toes into the grass for better traction. Slowly, straining and heaving, one team eventually dragged the other across the finish line, and as you might expect, the winning teams were almost always better sports about it than the losers.

The rest of the day would be a long hot battle between the Cadillacs and the Ramblers, or the Tigers and the Wildcats, or the Spartans and the Trojans, depending on which year it was. Bitty little kids balanced boards on their heads and walked as fast as they could and ran relay races, mostly in the right direction.

Bigger kids biked as slowly as they could

and jumped rope as long as they could, but Sandy always won that one because the couples turning the rope got tired before she did. The biggest kids leaped over hurdles, high jumped with awkward scissors kicks, and landed on everything from their faces to their buns in the long jump sawdust pit. Through it all, parents and proud "aunts" and "uncles" cheered as if a world record was at stake.

I was particularly worried about the high jump my senior year, since I hadn't really practiced for it. Towner and I had been cruising the center a couple months before looking for something to do one night and happened on the school's trampoline. Towner was a great tramp jumper and I was mediocre and we jumped doubles for a while and then did some experimenting.

"Have you ever done a seat flip?" Towner asked.

"No, how do you do it?" I should have had him go first.

"You do a seat drop and push with your hands a little and flip right over."

I did a seat drop, pushed a little with my hands, flipped right over about halfway and landed on my head. There was a loudish crack, the world spun in dark brown circles and I couldn't breath. I didn't see any light at the end of a long tunnel, but I remember that Towner kind of laughed, which is probably what I would have done in his shoes. Not that he wore shoes.

"Get Aunt Anita," I gasped, wanting someone besides Towner to witness my last words. Aunt Anita was in the children's home across the road.

Thankfully my breath returned on its own and I didn't have to think of anything memorable to say, but I noticed a pretty sharp pain in my back for the next few days and eventually trudged up to the clinic for an X-ray. Cracked vertebra. What a bother.

"So what does that mean?" I asked the doctor, not really wanting to know.

"It means don't do anything very active for about six weeks," he answered, and I assumed that meant I shouldn't practice for the high jump.

My first jumps of the year were therefore in front of a whole crowd of spectators, and when I won the blue ribbon I decided that what I really needed before a major competition is a long rest rather than intense practice — a philosophy I've tried to implement ever since. I've never tried the seat flip again.

Field days always ended at the lake where swimmers dog-paddled their way to victory, some swimming nearly the whole way underwater and shocking everyone with their progress when they came up for air ahead of the pack. Divers performed aerial acrobatics that roughly fit into categories like swan dive, gainer, front flip and jackknife. One point for landing in the water instead of on the raft. One point for making the swan dive look like anything better than a condor attack. One point for getting the jack knife opened back up before you hit the water. Etc.

We all learned that winning is relative — you didn't have to be great, you just had to be better than the guy who landed on his beet red belly right before you went in face first, 3/4 of the way through a flip and a half. There was certainly lots of room for good sportsmanship on the diving boards.

Refreshed and exhausted, we ended the day with a final tally of the team totals and hoarse cheers from the winners, thankful that we wouldn't have to do any of that stuff again until the next year. For my last field day I ended up with a 3x5 index card that had a tin foil star and five ribbons and said,

TIGERS, Ronny Snell, December 1, 1967

Dash
*2nd*

High Jump
*1st*

Hurdles
*1st*

Swimming
*3rd*

Long Distance
*2nd*

Fortunately you can't tell from the card how many kids I was competing against. Not that anyone cared, of course, since winning wasn't all that important and we were just one big happy family. Whatever.

# Chapter 12
## *Graduation*

We stood at the back of the auditorium, our borrowed blue gowns hot in the muggy evening. Snug blue caps smashed our freshly cut hair and gold tassels swung nervously as we waited to walk down the center aisle. Our shoes, rarely worn, squished feet shaped like paddles. We wouldn't have worn them even tonight, but the graduation announcements had specifically included a plea for the graduates to wear shoes, so we did. In front of me was my friend Tim Hawkins, or "Shawnk." Behind me was my brother

Terry. The whole graduating class of 1968, in alphabetical order. Everyone else was on furlough.

It was an historic moment — we were the first graduates to have had all of our schooling, starting with kindergarten, at Yarinacocha. Minus a couple years out for furloughs, of course. We were the first graduates to wear caps and gowns, borrowed from a private school in Lima. Our theme, plastered on the wall behind the stage in silver letters, was "Climbing the Heights." Mural sized mountains and trees symbolically showed the heights we were climbing. To the left of the stage, an American flag. To the right, a Peruvian flag.

Aunt Lydia began pounding out the processional on the black upright piano that had accompanied our worship services all my life. Our hearts pounded right along as the 8th graders went first, boys in white shirts and dark ties. Four years behind us, they were nevertheless all close friends — a crazy bunch of kids that included my sister Sandy.

I'm not sure why graduation from 8th grade was so special. Maybe it was because we'd never had a high school graduation before. Anyway, the audience stayed seated while all eleven of them walked the aisle. And then it was our turn.

"Pomp and Circumstance," even in the

jungle. Everyone please rise. We walked slowly down the aisle, centers of attention and proud smiles, climbed the heights to the stage, stood in front of a lifetime of friends, "aunts" and "uncles", the only family we had ever really known, special saints in flesh and blood and a few warts.

Mr. James gave the invocation before Mrs. Sawyer sang the Star Spangled Banner. No one sang the Peruvian national anthem, which says something about the confused mixture of cultures that we were graduating from. Ironically, if the high schoolers had been asked to sing, they would have belted out the Peruvian national anthem with gusto.

The eighth graders went first. Presentation of the class, handing out of diplomas by Uncle Will, the chairman of the school board who had two of his own boys in the class, smiling recessional and seats with parents in the audience. The rest of the ceremony would be ours alone. My mind wandered around the campus I was about to leave, "alma mater," "foster mother."

Right behind me, attached to the back of the auditorium, was a little room where I did first and second grade. The most memorable thing about second grade was being too embarrassed to raise my hand to go to the bathroom and wetting my pants.

We moved from building to building

around the soccer field as we got older. Many of our teachers only came for a year or two, taking advantage of sabbaticals in the USA or just looking for a chance to serve God in a different setting. Most were outstanding, but standing out from all the rest of our elementary school teachers was Miss Vangie, a pretty single woman whom we fell in love with in 5th grade, and who fell in love with us.

Since we never had more than one girl in our class from K-12, it was easier for us to fall in love with pretty single women than with handsome single men, not that there were any. I'm not sure what was so special about Miss Vangie besides being pretty. A special interest in each of us? An enthusiastic joy? I can't even remember anything specific that she taught us, but I do remember getting bitten by a snake I was trying to catch in the tree outside our classroom. A lot of us had snakes in our desks, but I guess this particular one wasn't interested.

In the next building over we did our wrestling for physical education, on kapok mats. That's how I got the only broken bone I've ever had. Danny Minor got my arm behind my back and just kept pulling up until it broke, which was a pretty good education physically. He won the match, if I remember correctly, and I went off to the clinic for X-rays and a sling. A nice clean break, right by the shoulder, so no itchy, scratchy, "can't swim for two months" cast. I think maybe the teacher/coach started blowing his whistle a little sooner after that. In the jungle, you kind of learn as you go.

We missed 7th and 8th grades at Yarinacocha while we were on furlough. By the time we got back we were ready to start high school, which kind of grew as we grew. When we needed ninth grade, they added ninth. When we were ready for tenth, they added tenth. Looking back, even with almost thirty years of perspective, I can't imagine a better place to go to high school, nor better friends to do it with. We had it all.

Of course, having it all didn't exactly mean we really had it all to perfection. For example, our sports program consisted mainly of soccer scrimmages on a little field that had a pretty bad slope to it. One good downhill kick and you were suddenly in track and field, chasing the ball between classrooms and palm trees, leaping over hurdles, doing some long jumps. We played some basketball too, but I don't remember much about that. There must have been some rules, but I don't remember what they were. I think the sports program actually picked up steam after we graduated, with tennis courts, real basketball, slam bang volleyball and even Saturday afternoon softball for the old men in their thirties and forties.

One of the genuinely unique and refreshing parts of our high school was that there was a steady influx of new teachers, each eager to explore what was to them a wonderfully new world. They brought a lot of creativity and new ideas each year and experimented on us more than they got to experiment on their kids back in the USA. Sometimes I think they were just having fun and they included us because they had to.

Mind you, the jungle is a great place to have classes. Imagine a biology class with your own 16-foot anaconda. One afternoon Mr. Fitch wanted a picture of the anaconda showing how long it really was. It took six of us to hold it more or less stretched out, fighting against muscles that felt like steel cables. It was a pretty good challenge keeping it fed, given that it mostly liked things like live possums, dogs, cats, rabbits and other household pets.

Our insect collections included peanut bugs and rhinoceros beetles. On our field trips we could actually get bitten by things most kids just get to see in pictures. I even remember tromping through jungle and mud one hot day to estimate the distance across Lake Yarinacocha for a geometry class. It was a fabulously practical application of triangulation and I'm sure we were accurate to within about two miles.

Because we had such a small school, everyone got to participate in everything. We never had to worry about the humiliation of tryouts. Want to be in the school play? You're in. The school choir? Have a seat. The basketball team? If you weren't on the team there wasn't a team! The high school cantata? I hate to think of it.

I had to sing a solo in the cantata my senior year. It had one note that I couldn't possibly reach and I hit it flat every practice. I dreaded performance night when I'd get to go flat in front of the whole center, but Martha Shanks rescued me. As I stood singing my heart out, she waited next to me, counting the beats in anticipation. The crucial moment came and she whacked me on the leg. "NOW," she whispered loudly enough to overpower my singing. I'm told I hit that note right on the money, my face contorted with the effort.

That was more gracious of Martha than you might think. In Spanish class we shared a teacher with another class. When Mrs. Peckham left our room to attend to theirs, we had a great time tying Martha's waist-long hair to the back of her chair so she couldn't sit up straight. Besides, we were merciless when she practiced her violin — howling like wolves and yelling for her to quit strangling the monkey. Martha, I must admit, didn't owe me any favors.

Yup, we had it all. We even had a president, vice president and secretary of the high school, complete with campaign managers and heated campaigning that included posters, slogans and speeches. Not that we didn't already know everything about everybody but it was still a good opportunity to make extravagant claims and empty promises, which was great preparation for politics in the USA.

I was president my senior year. Although it wasn't the highest office in the world, it did qualify me to welcome the President of Peru when he landed in his helicopter on our soccer field. I had been thoroughly briefed on what to say when I stepped up to shake President Belaunde's hand but as usual it completely slipped my mind. Thankfully he was an extremely gracious gentleman and made me feel that whatever I said was exactly right.

After I had formally welcomed him, President Belaunde stepped out of his chopper and we all sang the Peruvian national anthem. Diplomatic as ever, he asked us to sing the Star Spangled Banner for him. Unfortunately none of us knew the words except the teachers, so it sounded a little thin just as it had when we tried to sing it for two visiting senators from the USA. I introduced them during a school assembly, although I can't remember who they were or why they were there.

The blurb in the school annual says that we were an industrious set of officers whose main accomplishments were a fifteen minute break in the morning, the issuing of school pennants, planning for chapel, ditch-day and parties, which included a box social to raise money, a Freshman Initiation Day, a "spooky" Halloween party, Hat Day and Slave Day. I also arranged for caps and gowns for graduation, not realizing how hot they would be while we were waiting to give our speeches.

As I sat on the same stage where I had recently recited all of *The Midnight Ride of Paul Revere* during a speech contest, scanning the same audience, I spotted Uncle Jim taking pictures from the right side of the auditorium, about a third of the way back. If there was any one person who had defined my high school years, who had broadened my interests, who had challenged me to climb the heights, it was Uncle Jim, barefoot even for graduation.

Uncle Jim had taught me geometry and industrial arts from his craft shop just across the soccer field from the auditorium.

We were best of friends, traveling around Peru in his old white Ford pickup, spending hours together in the craft shop, sailing the lake in his little dinghy. He had taught me to take pictures and how to process them in his photo lab. He had shown me how to cut a tiger's eye and set it in a silver ring for my sister. He had helped me make cabinets for our bathroom in the house that he himself had built fifteen years before. He had let me work on the big catamaran he was building for a trip down the Amazon and up through the Caribbean. One berth would be in the aft section of the starboard hull, he had said, reserved for me.

We built clunky go-carts out of old engines in Uncle Jim's shop, formed clay sculptures on his pottery wheel and wired a house for practical electrical experience. We lifted weights on his bench press following routines he designed and learned basic gymnastics moves on rings and bars. If it could be done, he could do it — a jack of all trades and master of most. He became a grandpa during my senior year and was disgusted by how old it made him sound until we told him it was humiliating for us to be continually outdone by a grandfather. Then he wore it as a badge of honor.

Uncle Jim had said over and over that if you could read English and understand it, you could learn to do anything. He proved it. Many evenings in the children's' home he studied correspondence courses (nautical design, accounting, whatever) accompanied by Peter Paul and Mary or Alpine yodeling or Caribbean calypso or western ballads by Marty Robbins. His music tastes were international and included everything except mindless rock and roll.

I often went to Uncle Jim with questions about how to do things.

"Here," he'd say, "read this." I would.

"I'm not sure what it means."

"Read it again."

"I did."

"Read it again. If you can read and understand English, you can learn to do anything." To this day, when I want or need to learn something new, I buy or borrow a few books and read, and read again, and read again. It was the most important thing I learned in high school.

Uncle Jim rarely gave a compliment. I vividly remember the day I ended up in Iquitos, a city in northern Peru, unexpectedly having to spend a long day with nothing but my camera. I went for a walk, snagged what I thought would be a great picture and took it back to Yarina. Late one afternoon I developed and printed it in Uncle Jim's darkroom and set my small print out to dry.

Early the next morning when I went to

collect my picture, there were 10 prints of it spread out on the table, the biggest ones poster size.

"I thought it was pretty good," he said. I still have the picture, and the lump in my throat.

Abruptly my mind was jerked back to the stage on which we were being officially presented as the graduating class of 1968 and introduced for our speeches. All three of us spoke, of course. After all, in a class of three, you can't just have a valedictorian and a salutatorian. I went first, talking about the physical aspects of climbing the heights. Terry and Shawnk followed with the emotional and spiritual aspects. I don't have a clue what I said, much less what they said. Presumably we all said something immortal, even if we can't remember it.

Uncle Will handed us our diplomas, shaking each hand and hitting each of us with the special twinkle he had in his eye. Favorite uncle, so to speak. Then a special number by Aunt Grace, who had made corsages of homegrown orchids and gardenias for the graduate's mothers. My own mother was quite proud to be the mother of 2/3 of the graduating seniors and an eighth grade graduate all in the same night. One of Aunt Grace's daughters was my girlfriend at the time and her other daughter had just graduated from kindergarten in the morning. At

Yarinacocha, that was about as significant as graduating from high school.

I'm not sure why the program called for us to sing an emotional hymn at such an emotional time. We could have used some comic relief about now — something along the lines of "Over the river and through the woods, climbing the heights we go...." Instead, the whole audience rose for "He Leadeth Me," printed on the back of the program as if there was anyone there who could read the words through their tears.

> He leadeth me, Oh blessed thought,
> Oh words with heavenly comfort fraught.
> What e'er I do, where e'er I be,
> Still tis God's hand that leadeth me.

Voices were cracking. The words were fraught with heavenly comfort, but we all knew that once this ceremony was over we would leave behind everything we had known and loved, and head for a country that felt nothing like home. On we sang into the chorus, confident in God, not at all confident in anything else.

> He leadeth me, He leadeth me,
> By His own hand He leadeth me.
> His faithful follower I would be,
> For by His hand He leadeth me.

God's leading at the moment was taking me to Moody Bible Institute in the cold concrete jungle of Chicago, which I pretty much dreaded. I had decided to get a year of Bible training before I transferred to another school for a teaching credential in industrial arts. In a nutshell, at 16 years of age, I wanted nothing so much as to be another Uncle Jim.

On the way to college, Terry and I would stay in Elkhart, Indiana with Charles and Jaxie Miller, who had generously and bravely written to invite us. We vaguely remembered him as our Sunday school teacher during our last furlough, but for all practical purposes we weren't enthusiastic about having to stay with someone we didn't know.

The high school chorus sang a special number in our honor and Uncle Cecil, Shawk's dad, gave a message that I don't remember any better than I do my own. Mr. Peckham, chemistry teacher, pronounced a benediction and high school was over — a collection of pictures, a collage of memories, a world gone by.

In the morning we dressed back up graduate style and took more collectible pictures under the palm trees. Terry and me with Melody, Terry and me with Sandy, Terry and me with Mom, Terry and me with Dad, tall me with short Verna the kindergarten graduate.

"I'm so proud of you," my dad told me between pictures, hugging. "I'm so proud of you." He didn't say it often, but then I didn't say very often how proud I was of him, either. It was a good time to catch up.

Finally a picture of the whole family. Now the whole family again. And again, as if taking pictures would somehow keep us together forever.

"Life is a Jungle!"

# Chapter 13
## *The Graduation Gift*

Dear Ronny,

For your graduation gift we are giving you an all-expenses-paid trip from Yarinacocha to Mantaro, Kompiroshiato, Quillabamba, Machu Picchu, Cuzco, Lake Titicaca and Lima, with Dad and Uncle Jim. Have fun!

Love, Dad and Mom

"All expenses paid" in my family meant we wouldn't be eating much and we'd be sleeping on some pretty hard floors and I couldn't even tell if this was an expression of love or another attempt to get rid of me, but it didn't matter — a trip is a trip. Terry got a similar note and we were overjoyed. After all, apart from the wonder of finally getting to see Machu Picchu and Cuzco, we'd actually get to land on the Mantaro airstrip, which was a sport sufficiently life-threatening to inspire anyone. Besides, there was always the adventure of not knowing quite how we'd get from Kompi to Quillabamba — obviously Dad was planning this trip instead of Mom.

A sense of eager anticipation carried us through the black days we spent packing, cleaning out our rooms, selling anything we could to our sisters and friends for exorbitant prices, saying good-bye to everyone we knew, taking pictures as if they might somehow take the place of the place. It was turning out to be painfully hard packing all of our lives into two suitcases apiece.

The day after graduation, 44 of our friends left on one flight to Lima and the USA — a massive furlough exodus that left the Pucallpa airport ankle deep in muddy tears. Until a similar influx of people returned at the end of the summer, Yarinacocha would be a ghost town.

Our own packing was briefly interrupted on June 18, when 65 military attaches from all over South America came to tour

Yarinacocha, which undoubtedly set a record for the most polished shoes ever worn on our center at one time. It made me kind of want to bend down and put a little dust on a shoe just so I could see a general go to pieces.

The shiny shoes and gleaming medals were split into two groups, with a guide and a helper for each group. Terry and I were both helpers, which probably means we were about the only people left on the center. As helpers we were supposed to "be available to sub-divide the groups and make any appropriate remarks as necessary." Although I'm sure it was an awesome occasion I don't remember much of it and I especially don't remember making any appropriate remarks, though I can't imagine not being tempted.

For the luncheon in our dining room a bunch of us kids dressed up in native costumes to act as waiters and waitresses, sort of like a circus side show. I wore a Machiguenga cushma, of course, but had on a pair of baggy old cutoffs underneath with no belt.

We were all pretty jittery since everyone on the center was trying to make a good impression on our guests, who sat around the tables in starchy uniforms that had all kinds of impressive things hanging on them. I felt awful when I dropped a fork on the floor right beside some pretty heavy brass.

I felt even worse when I bent down to pick up the fork and felt the old clasp in my cutoffs pop loose. *Oh no*, I thought, *not now*! The zipper on those wretched shorts didn't stay up very well on its own and as I stood back up I could tell I was going to lose my shorts. I looked toward the kitchen, my only escape, and could barely see it far over the horizon. Both hands were occupied with a heavy tray. Time for a strategic retreat, but how?

I pasted a grim smile on my red face and started carefully away from the tables. By spreading my knees apart I could slow my shorts' descent somewhat but I couldn't stop it and I didn't dare run. Even walking stealthily I felt them falling, centimeter by centimeter. Halfway there a cook saw me and stopped long enough to stare and whisper something to a girl in a securely tied grass skirt. Big question marks formed on their amused faces but I looked right past them and kept going, feet spreading with each step.

By the time I reached the kitchen I walked as if I had a full load in my pants, but the pants were around my ankles like hobbles. The attaches, we were told later, loved the luncheon and thought the service was splendid. But... was that boy okay?

On Monday morning, July 8th, we collected at our own little hangar, where we had said good bye to friends dozens of times over the years as we or they headed for scattered villages. This time would be different — it wasn't for a couple weeks, nor for a few months, but forever. The pilot prayed for our safety, something we took very seriously when we'd be in a wheel plane over hundreds of miles of nothing but jungle and rivers. In a float plane, we actually *wished* for an engine failure just so we'd have a great story to tell but landing in a river in a wheel plane is a bit more drastic.

We kissed and hugged the handful of family and friends who had come to see us off, then the four of us folded our legs into a little Helio Courier with the pilot and fastened shoulder and lap belts. Mom and Sandy and Melody would fly directly to Lima to meet us. We hadn't a clue when we would see the rest of our wellwishers again. By bending my head down a bit and crinking my neck, I could look out the scratchy plexiglass window. The pilot yelled "LIBRE" for Spanish speakers and "CLEAR" for English speakers and turned the key.

"Know what that engine's for?" he shouted as the engine sputtered to life and then revved smoothly for a few minutes.

"What?" we asked obligingly.

"It's to keep the pilot cool. You should see him sweat when it stops."

We'd heard that little joke dozens of times but we nevertheless laughed politely. Tears started to flood my eyes. My stomach was in a tight knot. "He leadeth me, oh blessed thought," we had sung at graduation just days ago. Now it felt as if He was leading me in entirely the wrong direction.

A cool breeze blew through the vents, evaporating the sweat that drenched us. The pilot pulled and turned the stick to make sure that flaps and rudders and other things moved when they were supposed to and didn't move when they weren't supposed to, then checked a few switches and flipped through his checklist for takeoff. I'd watched them go through it so many times I felt as if I could've done it myself.

Uncle Jim had actually been a jungle pilot back in the days when they could sort of make up their own rules. Once things got more organized he felt too restricted and bowed out. For example, he didn't like not being able to buzz his house to let Aunt Anita know he was home. He still enjoyed flying, but had to settle for the copilot's seat.

"And don't kick that valve," the pilot reminded him, pointing to the fuel cutoff valve down by his leg, "or things will get a little exciting."

We taxied down the length of the runway. The engine revved again and spun us around, facing into the wind. 11:35 a.m.

"Everyone ready?" the pilot shouted.

No. I would never be ready for this. But of course I couldn't say so. You do what you must and hope your emotions will eventually catch up with your commitment. I had seen my parents do it a hundred times. They did it as they left cold Chicago to come to muggy Yarinacocha in 1950. Now it was my turn, leaving muggy Yarinacocha to go to cold Chicago 18 years later.

We surged forward, gaining speed until the tail wheel lifted off, and then the main wheels and surprisingly quickly we climbed toward the heavens, ears depressurizing, airplane bouncing slightly in the wind. Through blurry eyes I caught glimpses of the hangar, of the people waving far below, of the swim ramp and the raft where my friends lay sunbathing, of our house overlooking the beautiful lake. It was like looking at a water color painting, all of the images and colors melting together. I hunkered down and stared out the window, waiting for the pain in my throat to ease, feeling my heart breaking, not wanting the others to see.

Fortunately, it's hard to mourn for long

in a Helio. We climbed past the soaring buzzards and then into brilliant, billowing clouds. Since some of those clouds topped out at 25-30,000 feet and had powerful updrafts inside them, we zoomed between and around them, banking this way and that, instead of flying through them. Riding a roaring updraft would've been exhilarating, but coming back down with no wings would've been more exhilaration than any of us was ready for.

We leveled off above most of the clouds, where the sun shone brightly, and hoped that our bladders would make it the whole way — the one all-consuming thought on every flight in a small plane. Through holes in the clouds we could see endless jungle and rivers that twisted like snakes, sometimes almost completely looping back on themselves.

"Pity any poor fool trying to make this trip by river," I thought, and then remembered that I had done it voluntarily twice already. And would probably do it again, given the chance. Two hours by plane. Two weeks by boat.

An hour and a half into our flight, as we napped, the radio went out. After trying everything he could except kicking it (pilots don't kick things in airplanes, especially at 9,000 feet), the pilot finally announced the bad news.

"Looks like we've got to turn around. I can't go on without my radio." Sounded like some teens I know. Getting out to check the battery connections was sort of out of the question.

Pilots flying over the jungle called in to our linguistic center every fifteen minutes or so with progress reports. In case of a forced landing, searchers would know more or less where to hunt for the wreckage. Otherwise the little plane could disappear into the enormous canopy of trees without leaving a trace. Although we didn't want to go back, neither did we particularly want to vanish without a trace, no matter how good a story it would have made.

After a half hour of going the wrong direction, the radio perversely started working again on its own. We retraced the route we had just retraced, which was great news except that we'd just added an hour to our bladder time. You could see legs squeezing together and teeth clenching. This is the part about missionary work that you'll never read in prayer letters but believe me, people pray pretty earnestly when they make the mistake of drinking too much before takeoff.

Our first stop was Camisea, where the pilot ambled over to the fuel drums and the rest of us sprinted for the bushes. It was always a little embarrassing when

Machiguengas came to meet us at the plane and we ran right past them into the jungle, but first things first.

There was a lot of sickness going around in Camisea and many of the people had tried to flee the flu by running into the jungle, unfortunately taking it with them farther and farther away from medical help. Dad spent some time talking to the school teacher and the village head man, updating them, getting updated and taking orders for goods and services and school materials, which were always in short supply.

We helped the pilot fill the tanks in the wings, said goodbye to our special friends individually and crunched ourselves back in for the hop to Picha, where we had lived when Mom got hepatitis and the roof fell in. Not that there was any connection.

Mario ran up from the river to greet us, still about 5' tall and still with legs that looked like parentheses and still with a nose that looked as if he'd run into a tree going about forty miles an hour. Dad spent another half hour doing the same things with him that he'd done in Camisea.

"We're going now, Brother," we said. "We'll come back."

"I'll be dead by then," he answered. It was a common farewell for the Machiguengas, whose lives were terribly precarious and we all knew it might be true. Mario was one of our very first friends, a brother indeed, with a mischievous sparkle in his eye and gold rimmed teeth in his smile. I would miss him.

It was drizzling now. Low gray clouds, silently weeping.

"It looks a little better over toward Mantaro," said the pilot cheerfully after he'd reported by radio that we were off the ground at Picha at 1630. We hoped so. Mantaro's airstrip was the worst in the mountainous jungle and it wouldn't be a whole lot of fun landing on it if we couldn't see it. On the other hand, there were some people who closed their eyes as they landed there, so it wouldn't make that much difference to them. I think the pilots kept their eyes open all the time but I'm just guessing.

The foothills of the Andes rose up to meet us. We could see bright red trees in bloom, bamboo thickets that stretched for miles like weeds, even pairs of macaws flying below us. And then suddenly the airstrip was underneath us — a tiny 250-yard scar of bare dirt with the winding river and a row of thatched houses curving around one end and up one side, thick jungle on the other side and a steep mountain at the far end. It was a great airstrip for people who liked adrenaline rushes.

We flew high over the strip once to make sure no one had built a house in the middle of it and there were no big animals or people on it. Once we started our blind approach, we would be committed for better or worse and it wouldn't do to suddenly discover someone's room addition in our sights.

"Well, it looks good," said the pilot with a massive dose of exaggeration. He was either trying to encourage us or he had his eyes shut. "Everybody buckled up?" We were indeed and hanging on with white knuckles. Uncle Jim had his camera smashed against his face for the last-minute photos that never showed much but gave him something to think about besides his wife and kids.

We flew back downriver, losing altitude and the pilot tensed as he banked sharply into the river bed and slowed us down to a flutter. We descended into the narrow slot between the trees, our ears popping, the airstrip hidden up around the bend. All we could see was a massive 400-ton boulder blocking the right side of the airstrip. The Machis had done everything they could to break up or move that boulder but there it still sat, daring us to hit it.

We swerved left around the boulder and the slats on the fronts of the wings banged down to keep us from stalling and the wheels hit the ground and we bounced slightly and skidded to a stop and we hadn't hit the boulder and we hadn't gone off into the river and we hadn't ploughed into the mountain or the jungle and oh thank You God! Sometimes it's so *good* to be alive!

"That's a doozie, isn't it?" laughed the pilot as he picked up his microphone to report us on the ground at Mantaro at 1715 for the night. Everyone on both ends let out a huge sigh of relief and turned off their radios.

We climbed out into a throng of wide-eyed Machis who wore ragged cushmas and bright red face paint and necklaces of seeds and teeth and bones and ancient Peruvian coins and caps from toothpaste tubes. Hmmm... those toothpaste tube caps must have been introduced by the Incas. Their robes smelled like campfire smoke, the smell of home to us, and their long black hair stuck out in every direction.

One man came forward with a big smile, a bulge of coca leaves in one cheek, a few stained teeth and a handful of black walnuts as a gift. We worked our way along the crowd and eventually ended up at Venturo's house for a supper of manioc, boiled fish and bananas. Full and at home, Terry and I sat down beside someone's fire to roast walnuts and talk to them long into the night. 7:30, to be exact.

A full moon blasted through the clouds off and on, bathing the whole valley in bright light. The river sparkled silver as it roared past, and I thought to myself each time I woke up to change positions on the hard palm floor that there couldn't be a more beautifully picturesque village on earth.

In the morning Venturo fixed us pancakes and syrup, which is a little like flying into the Sahara desert and having someone fix you fresh trout. Then everyone gathered in the school for a church service, complete with singing and a message from Dad.

Although I know God loved that singing and considered it an act of joyful worship, I'd have to say it was pretty hard to keep a straight face and I can't even come close to describing it. But I'll try:

There were 50 or 60 Indians with a good mixture of men and women and children. Some of them apparently couldn't carry a tune at all. Some of the others could clearly carry a tune but they each sang in a different octave or key and just sang their hearts out without regard for what anyone else was singing. Only a few knew the words.

Venturo started the song: "Jesus loves me…Itakena Kirishito." Actually, that's "Christ loves me" — since "Jesus" doesn't have enough syllables to fill up the lines in Machi. He of course sang really loud, mostly so that he could hear himself above the coming bedlam and not get distracted. A few people, having already learned something about group singing, joined him.

After three or four notes several women chimed in with high squeaky voices — almost falsetto. Although they started a little late, they started at the beginning of the song, not wanting to miss a single word. After they got a bit of a head start a few old men began to bellow a different tune in a different key. There's just no kinder way to say it. Of course they didn't want to miss anything either, so they also started at the beginning even though Venturo was now halfway through the first stanza.

Terry and I were trying our best to keep up with Venturo but we started giggling and couldn't stop. That may sound immature, but if Mom had been there she wouldn't have looked at anyone, including us, because then she'd have started giggling and wouldn't have been able to stop. Dad, on the other hand, just joined right in not knowing the difference since he was one of the ones who couldn't carry a tune or follow a beat. He was just glad to be in a place where no one cared how he sang, or how loud.

Soon it was a race. The women with the

high squeaky voices gained speed and passed up Venturo, who maintained a pretty consistent tempo in the face of severe odds. The old men wore out and started dragging. Somehow they persevered all the way through the first verse, finishing it well after Venturo had launched into the second.

Dad was still going strong with a tune that must have come straight from the Spirit, and when it was all over we each finished at our own pace, with one or two old men slowly bringing up the rear, right through to the last word. Uncle Jim was hiding his chuckles behind his camera, but I could see his shoulders and stomach shaking.

All in all, I'd have to say a pond full of bullfrogs and a herd of just-weaned calves and a tree full of parrots could do better but I know God loved it and I know the Machis loved him. Apart from the fact that I couldn't keep from laughing, it was an awesome time of worship and I was humbled by their new faith.

Once we had survived the singing we walked upriver to see a famous Mantaro bridge. The Machis had made it by bending saplings across the 60-foot wide river from each side and then sort of lacing them together with vines and more branches like a bird's nest. They climbed on it and raced across and didn't get all that concerned about the fact that it creaked and groaned and trembled and swayed and shook and pieces of it fell into the river. We climbed on it and inched along and thought to ourselves that it would be a lot less dangerous to just swim across the torrent below without having to fall off the bridge first.

We had to leave Mantaro in two trips, since the airstrip was so short. Terry and Dad climbed in just before noon and Venturo called the people to come for prayer. They did, and prayed together for our strength and safety along the way. The fruit of the ministry, blessing us in return.

We landed in Kompi on the airstrip B.C. and I had slaved over three years earlier. Now there were two villages in the area, each with its own school. Sadly the teachers, both named Pedro, weren't particularly getting along. Pedro V. had recently reported that he'd heard that Pedro R. was getting drunk, beating school children, kicking people, pulling hair, scolding the adults as if they were children, forcing men to work in his fields but not sharing the produce, and making the people so angry they were threatening to leave the community and scatter back into the jungle. According to the stories, two men had drowned because of his abuse.

When Pedro R. told his side of the story,

it was naturally quite the opposite, expressing surprise that people were saying this of him when he had done so much to teach them and work with them. As far as he knew, the people didn't want any other teacher and had in fact told him that if he didn't continue on as the teacher they would just all leave. And the two men who drowned? One was drunk and the other was killed by a husband whose wife had been involved in an affair.

So did he or did he not pull hair out of men's heads and legs out of girls' sockets? Probably not, but stories and rumors would continue, undermining the sense of unity that the fledgling communities needed to survive. The Machis got involved in petty jealousies and power conflicts as easily as we do and besides, they were still trying to figure out what schools and villages and living together was really all about.

Pedro V. himself, once courageous and unselfish and firmly committed to applying the Scriptures to Machi life, had apparently drifted into the more familiar role of village boss, drinking too much manioc beer and building his power base however he could, capitalizing on false rumors.

The pilot said something along the lines of "Be warmed and fed" and then abandoned us, undoubtedly grateful that he didn't have to go on our special trip.

There were a lot of people who didn't think our trips were all that special. Like right at the moment there was hardly anybody in Kompi and we didn't know how we were going to go on. Most importantly, Pedro V., the same school teacher I had worked with in Kompi three years earlier, was living somewhere downriver. Of course he hadn't known we'd be coming.

Someone fed us a stick of boiled manioc for lunch and then a young man volunteered to take us to Pedro's house. We hoisted our flour sacks full of stuff over our shoulders and followed him through the little village.

For an hour and a half we slid along a slippery trail that followed and crossed the shallow river. Terry and I, barefoot like our guide, fared better than Dad and Uncle Jim. Their useless shoes skidded out from under them and left them thrashing for balance until our guide must have wondered if they'd been drinking too much on the plane.

About the time we were ready to collapse we saw two Machis poling a canoe up the river. They happily let us climb in, turned around and headed back downriver as if they had nothing to do upriver anyway. For our part, we happily got out and walked whenever we came to a rapid, since they obviously hadn't been using canoes all that long and we didn't particularly want them practicing on us.

By suppertime we were at Pedro and Adela's house, soaking wet. While they eagerly soaked up news of the outside world we dried our clothes beside their fire. Even now, in the midst of all their problems and failures, I loved and admired them, my brother and his wife. I couldn't be very judgmental knowing that... well... they were just a lot like me and I hadn't a clue how I'd hold up under the pressures they'd faced.

We reminisced happily about the hard days of building the airstrip together. Adela fixed us a supper of manioc and fish and it was good to see that the menu hadn't changed in the past three years. The drink she served was... uhhh... a bit on the zingy side and we had uncomfortable thoughts of someone chewing manioc and spitting it into a little tub so it could ferment slightly before she mixed it with river water and handed it to us in enamel bowls. Although one little sip wasn't exactly enough to be polite in their culture, it was quite enough in ours.

We went to sleep with the happy news that there was a brand new canoe waiting for us downriver. *See, these things always work out*, we smiled naively to ourselves. We should have known better.

# Chapter 14

## *The Farewell*

Early in the morning we got up to wolf down a breakfast of vegetable and beef stew with bananas. We would use two rafts to go a short way downriver, then pick up a brand new canoe to go the rest of the way down the Kompiroshiato River to where it met the Urubamba.

Balsa rafts are fabulous in theory and not quite so fabulous in practice. Ours were made from seven or eight logs about seven inches in diameter and 16 feet long, not that the logs were all the same size or length. That would have been far too convenient. In the middle of the raft two stakes had been pounded in to form a cross about 18" off the floor. That was where we would lash our gear, high above the splashing waves. At least in theory.

To reduce weight, the heavy bark had all been peeled off, exposing a coating that was rather like mucous. You never get to feel that slimy stuff when you buy your balsa in hobby shops, but believe me, riding through a bouncy rapid on mucous-slick logs with no seat belt makes for a pretty good adventure, especially since rafts aren't all that easy to steer.

Although it was a barrel of fun, we would all feel a bit more secure when we got to the canoe. One more time we said goodbye to our Machiguenga friends and to their beautiful section of the jungle. By evening we would be back in the "white" man's world, a world that we considered civilization and the Machis considered nothing but dangerous.

We shoved off into the fast current, Terry and Dad ahead with two Indians and Uncle Jim and me behind with another two. The waves lapped at our ankles and the rocks bumped us this way and that and the sun slowly burned through the fog and we said to ourselves that this was the way life was meant to be lived.

Within half an hour we could see the

brand new canoe on the bank up ahead.
Funny thing about that brand new canoe —
it was so brand new it wasn't finished yet.
Dugout canoes that haven't been dug out
yet aren't a whole lot better than a raft. In
fact, they're a whole lot worse.

Now what? We had two options basically.
We could wait for the canoe to be finished,
in which case we'd have time to build a
house and plant a garden, or we could go on
with the our two little rafts.

Since Dad thought college was
important for us, we decided to juggle
things around a bit and use the rafts. Dad
and Uncle Jim ended up on one raft with a
Machi steerer and Terry and me on the
other with a steerer.

The two extra Indians walked back
upriver, which should have served as some
kind of warning, but didn't. I'm also not sure
why Dad and Uncle Jim got on the same
raft, but now I think it must had been the
better of the two rafts. After all, they were
both smart men.

The Kompiroshiato River isn't all that
big, but it's big enough to have some really
fun rapids all the way down it. It would
actually be easier to navigate in flood stage,
since then the water would cover most of the
rocks, but of course it wasn't in flood stage
and we didn't have enough faith to make it
rain right then. So we bounced and jolted

and slid on the slippery logs and it occurred to all of us that the Machi steerers we had hadn't been steering all that long. Apparently they had just come down out of the jungle and they were as excited about this trip as we were, which somehow wasn't much of an encouragement.

We managed several hours of joyful passage through remote jungle, passing no houses and seeing no other people. Terry and I got into the lead, though we were never far ahead, and when at noon we finally rounded the last bend to break out onto the Urubamba River, we were surprised not to see Dad and Uncle Jim behind us. We stretched out on a sand bar in the sun to wait, though it wasn't all that pleasant with the gnats biting and the sun acting pretty tropical.

We waited and waited and waited and eventually decided to go back upstream. Either something had gone wrong or they were eating all our food without us, and either way we wanted to be there.

In the end, something had gone wrong. We found them stretched out on their own sandbar, with all of our belongings stretched out with them. In the very last rapid their exuberant steerer, thrilled that he'd brought them the whole way without turning over, had gotten sideways to a big rock and lost control. The raft flipped up on its side, everyone hurtled overboard and the clever X-shaped luggage rack parted company with the raft. By the time we found them, Uncle Jim was holding his camera upside down so all the water could drain out, and he didn't look as if he could see the humor in the situation quite yet.

There wasn't a whole lot we could do but go on, so we crammed wet gear back into wet flour sacks, reboarded the rafts and floated down into the Urubamba River, which was much mightier and much more intimidating to the Machis. Fortunately we only had to go down it a short ways to find a trail that led up to a "white man's" house high above the river. We unloaded our stuff, said goodbye to our helpers and struggled up the steep bank.

Juan Olarte grew coffee and chocolate for a living and lived in relative filth off the proceeds. In fact, his house was so dirty that when he invited us to spend the night we opted to sleep out on the cement slab he used to dry his beans. Besides, it made a nice place to dry out our clothes, and in the afternoon sunshine Uncle Jim could take apart his camera with his pocket knife. Uncle Jim did those sort of things. I did too, but unlike my mentor I couldn't get them back together.

For supper we had a candy bar that we'd brought along and some hot, sticky, tasteless gruel that Mrs. Olarte prepared for us. We knew enough to be grateful and swallowed it all, though there's probably still a little stuck in my throat after all these years. Then, under a heavily overcast sky, we pulled damp blankets over us and more or less slept until 4:30.

For breakfast we had another minimally delightful meal of fried bananas and manioc and mountain coffee. Meaning they put a mountain of coffee in a cup and added a little water and it couldn't have been a whole lot stronger if we'd just injected it intravenously. I didn't much like it, but part of being polite was to drink it anyway, sort of like we'd done with Adela's toxic brew the night before.

By 5:30 we were on our way with a young Quechua boy for a guide. The trail started steeply into the mountains alongside the river, giving us the feeling that we might die right there and be glad we had. Fortunately it moderated after that initial steep burst and as the sun came over the mountains we had settled into a relatively good mule trail, used to carry produce up to where the road ended. Although the trail got better, we got worse. Terry and I walked barefoot and soon grew tired of the splintered rocks in the trail. At least it was better than having to wear shoes.

Uncle Jim's stomach was revolting over

the delicacies he'd been sending down, so he struggled to keep up without throwing up. By 10:00 we were all starved, but snacking on limes and sucking the white slime out of the chocolate bean pods didn't help. The sun, a warm and helpful friend in the early morning, became a blasting hot enemy as mid day approached.

Even when we got to the end of the road we had to keep walking, since there were no vehicles there. There are a lot of fun things I remember about this special trip, but that walk definitely wasn't one of them.

We arrived at a tiny little pigsty of a town called Sirialo around noon, and were overjoyed to find a truck just getting ready to leave for Quillabamba, where we hoped to spend the night. The driver said we could have a few minutes to eat lunch, which turned out to be a couple eggs apiece and some half cooked rice. Actually he wasn't being generous — he just needed time to drink a few more beers before we left.

We climbed into the back of the truck and perched ourselves on boards that spanned from side to side. The driver said it would take about five hours, but of course he didn't reckon on how thirsty he'd be along the way. We stopped four times so he could get something to eat, and double that so that he could have some more beer.

By about 5:00 the ride was getting a little

wobbly and the driver looked like a keg on legs.
I can't for the life of me figure out where he put
it all, but it wasn't reassuring as we zoomed
along right at the edge of sheer dropoffs. The
other passengers took it in stride and shared
their food with us, the best part of which was
a bag of little yellow potatoes that had been
smothered in mountain cheese. Since potatoes
originated in the mountains of Peru, those
Quechuas had a lot of good ideas of what to do
with them.

The five-hour ride turned into six, and
then seven and then eight on a rough dirt
road. It got really old bouncing along on the
hard wooden planks over rocks and across
shallow stream beds and we all wondered if
we would have any skin left on our
backsides when it was over.

Whenever we caught up to slower trucks,
our driver would pull right up behind them
on the one-lane road and blast his horn
while thick dust covered and filled us.
Sometimes that lasted for several miles
before the truck ahead pulled over to let us
by. When we finally rattled into
Quillabamba at 8:30, weaving and lurching,
the only difference between us and the
Quechuas was that we had blue eyes and
they had brown ones. Everything else was
dusty white.

We headed right for a hotel that didn't
cost much. Once we had set down our

smelly, dusty sacks, we found a restaurant that fed us steaks, french fries and rice with cold drinks. It was the first meal we'd had to pay for in a week of travelling, which is why Dad had offered to pay all expenses on this trip. After supper we crashed into creaky beds and lapsed into comas.

In the morning when we went to get train tickets, they were sold out. We were for all practical purposes stuck in Quillabamba, but decided to go on out to the train station anyway. Just hanging around might show up some options we hadn't considered yet, and there was always the option of just trying to get on without tickets. We bought some fruit and bread to carry us through whatever delays we might have ahead and hopped in the back of a truck for the ten-minute ride to the train station.

After asking a lot of questions and making a royal nuisance of ourselves, we discovered that we could take a dilapidated bus up the narrow-gauge tracks to Machu Picchu instead of the train. The bus's rubber wheels had been replaced with steel train wheels, but other than that it was still just an ancient city bus. We were happy to cram ourselves in with about twenty-five more people than there were seats. Heavy blue cigarette smoke filled the bus, and heavy black smoke billowed out behind it as we started off, everyone holding their baggage in their already crowded laps.

Our first stop was to fix the fuel pump and the second to fix the water pump, neither of which apparently liked going so steadily uphill. We were indeed climbing continuously from Quillabamba's jungle heat to Machu Picchu's mountain chill, and used other stops to refill the overheating radiator. Because the starter didn't work, after each repair several of us climbed out of the bus to push it backwards down the tracks until it started, then smashed ourselves back into the crowd for another couple hours of secondhand smoke. The whole time we wondered what might break down next or when a train might come from the other direction and not notice us until too late.

We pulled into the Machu Picchu train station at 3:30, the bus heaving and coughing and out of breath. With genuine relief we exited the smoky throng and found to our surprise that a brand new Mercedes bus would be down soon to take us to the ruins high above us. Of course first it would have to get over the narrow bridge across the Urubamba River — a bridge that hadn't apparently been built for such wide buses. Drivers took it all in stride, just folding their mirrors back so they wouldn't tangle with the suspension cables that held the bridge up.

As it turned out, the road to the ruins wasn't much wider than the bridge and as we traversed the thirteen switchbacks to the top of the mountain, we had splendid views out the windows of the bus. Why, we couldn't even see any road between us and the dropoffs, even if we stuck our heads out the windows. Some people in our family might not have been thrilled.

The tourist hotel beside the ruins was stunningly plush, especially compared to Juan Olarte's cement slab. Each room had its own bathroom, there was carpet on the floors, the restaurant was clean and bright. Terry and I had never seen such luxury, and thought it fabulous that we'd get to experience it. But of course we wouldn't; every bed was taken and there were no overflow rooms.

The manager was exceptionally nice to us, considering we looked as if we'd just crawled out of an armadillo hole and smelled like cigarette butts, but he really didn't have anything to offer. When we asked if we could sleep in one of his buses he said sure, but he wasn't sure he had any extra blankets. We thanked him, as grateful as Joseph and Mary when they were offered the stable, and headed out for our first look at the ruins in the late afternoon sunshine.

Since it was so late we didn't have to pay the 10 dollar entrance fee, but the man selling postcards at the front gate said we'd have to in the morning.

"They only make exceptions for people on special excursions," he explained, "but they have to get a letter in Cuzco saying that they're exempt." Dad of course immediately figured out that somehow that included us, even though we didn't fit any of the criteria. Dad was in fact a genius at figuring out how to include us in categories of people that didn't have to pay for things.

After wandering the ruins briefly and shivering in the cold we returned to the hotel to sit and talk with the manager and other guests. Everyone was awed by our trip and as helpful as could be. One couple was especially taken by our spirit of adventure.

"You can have our beds," they offered, "and we'll just sleep on the floor. Wait until after 10:30 though, when the electricity goes off." Apparently the management didn't like squatters, and especially squatters that didn't pay. We declined the invitation anyway, wanting to stick together in the bus.

By 9:00 we were once again hungry enough to eat anything in sight, which is the only reason we ate in the hotel restaurant. Not that the food was bad — we in fact feasted on soup, steak, potatoes, jello and an omelet apiece. The only thing wrong with it was the bill. We spend more on that one supper than we had for all beds, meals and transportation thus far. It was delicious, but since Dad hadn't reckoned on actually having expenses on this all expenses paid trip, we didn't eat there again.

After supper we hauled our thin blankets out to an old bus, where we found there wasn't any way to lie down comfortably. One of the drivers for the hotel soon popped his head in the door.

"I've left my new bus unlocked so you can sleep in it tonight," he said. "It's a lot more comfortable. Just wait until after 10:30 when the electricity goes off." We got the feeling that a lot of real life in Machu Picchu happened after 10:30, but by then we had figured out a way to get somewhat comfortable, and were fast asleep under a waning moon.

In the morning we got up at 5:30 so we could get sunrise pictures in the ruins, as opposed to staying in the bus shivering until the sun came up. Not that we would have had to rush — it took two more hours for the sun to come over the mountain peaks. By then my toes were totally numb and we had found a dozen cold wild strawberries to snack on. We hoped the picturesque llamas that roamed the ruins hadn't stopped anywhere near those bushes.

When the sun peeked over the peaks the temperature soared and our spirits with it. By midmorning we had seen the sun gate, the temple to the sun, the carefully crafted system of stone troughs and cisterns that brought running water right through the ancient city, the restored houses and a bunch of other things that people speculated had to do with religious ceremonies.

Since Machu Picchu had been abandoned before anyone from the outside found it, tour guides have more questions than answers. No one knew for sure why it had been built, nor what different parts of it were used for. Anything that didn't have an obvious use was immediately considered part of religious ceremonies. Someday I hope an Inca shows up to shed some light on their lives.

"A highly significant ceremonial rock that symbolizes the puma?" he'll laugh. "Naw, that was just something my boy carved in school and it was pretty ugly but my wife kept it because she never throws anything away. I think it was supposed to be a guinea pig."

About 10:30 a security officer approached.

"Can I see your entrance tickets?" he asked politely. We told him we didn't have any.

"You'll need to go get some, then," he said just as politely, and pointed us toward the front gate that we had bypassed in the early morning light.

Dad immediately went to work. He found the top man in charge and began a long torrent of carefully selected truths that included the fact that we had come in the back way from Quillabamba instead of Cuzco, we hadn't had opportunity to get the exemption papers, he was an anthropologist, Uncle Jim was a professor at Yarinacocha, Terry and I were students, we all worked for the Ministry of Education of Peru, and on and on until the poor man in charge decided we did indeed fit the right categories. Dad had provided him plenty to choose from, of course.

"You're welcome to go in free," he said handing us passes, "but please sign the special guest book when you leave." We said we'd be happy to do that.

Back in the ruins we headed for Huayna Picchu, a thousand-foot climb to a sharp peak that towers above Machu Picchu. For 35 minutes we puffed steadily upwards, then looked in awe at snowcapped peaks surrounding us, the river far below, the old terraces and buildings spread in front of us,

the jungle covered mountains that provide
Machu Picchu's magnificent backdrop. We
also chatted with a man and two girls who
had taken twice as long to get up there, in
part because one of the girls was afraid of
heights. She may have had no brains, but
she had guts.

After a lunch in the hotel, where we
borrowed a table and ate some of our fruit
and bread from Quillabamba, we took a bus
back down to the train station and got on a
tourist class train to go to Cuzco. Meaning
we each got a real seat to ourselves and
overhead racks for our bags, which didn't
look anything like the other bags on the
train.

For three hours we rumbled past the
turbulent foaming white water of the
Urubamba River, the snowy peak of Mt.
Veronica catching the last rays of the
setting sun, the fields and gardens where
Quechuas still ploughed with oxen. By the
time we reached the 12,000-foot pass above
Cuzco, the mighty river had dwindled to a
trickle we could step across. In a way we
were sad to leave it behind — it was
somehow a symbolic link to the Machi
villages where our friends still lived, totally
unaware of the world we now clattered
through.

As darkness fell we worked our way
down a series of switchbacks into Cuzco,

ooohing and aaahing over the splendid
array of city lights below us. Once at the
train station, the ooohing and aaahing was
quickly replaced by a mad scramble to get
rid of a hundred taxi drivers whose
livelihoods absolutely depend on us getting
into their cars, they each said.

We elbowed politely and pushed through
the throngs so we could walk to wherever
we were going, not that we had a clue where
that might be. As luck would have it, within
a couple of blocks we found a clean, new
hotel with bargain rates and hot showers. I
plunged in ahead of the rest.

It took about ten minutes to realize that
the showers weren't going to be hot after all.
I stripped and started shivering even before
I ducked under the spray, jumping and
shouting to ward off the hypothermia.
Within seconds my scalp was numb and I
could feel myself being taken over by
pneumonia, starting with my feet. I washed
as fast as I could, sprang out of the shower,
dressed and dove under the blankets to
warm up.

Uncle Jim, Captain Courageous, was
next. With none of the jumping or shouting
he got in and stayed in for a long, long time.
My respect rose another notch, until he
came out with a big smile.

"I think you had the wrong faucett
turned on," he laughed. "Thanks for saving

me some hot water."

We explored Cuzco, eating Peruvian food and taking pictures of what must be one of the most scenic cities on earth. We even got to see Uncle Jim dance at a restaurant after eating what looked like a sweet pepper and turned out to be a mouth melting firecracker. Tears rolled down his cheeks and I thought for a few minutes that he might even be human after all.

After Cuzco we took the train to Lake Titicaca and a bus to Lima, where Mom and Sandy and Melody were waiting for us. Our whole trip had taken ten days instead of two weeks, so somewhere along the line we hadn't had as much fun as we should have. Still, that gave us time to ride the taxis in Lima, go bowling, race go-carts and eat plate-sized steaks at Argentine steak houses. As fun as it was, a dark cloud began to descend on us as August third approached.

August third. D-Day. Though we tried not to mention it, tried to just ignore it, the calendar wouldn't stop for us. In some ways, I know what it's like to be on Death Row. Final visits, final meals, final pictures and requests. Attempts at lighthearted conversation, but always the inescapable feeling that something precious is about to be taken away.

We went out for dinner the night before,

not that anyone had an appetite. Back at our room in the guest house we went through the motions of a final packing. Our lifetimes hadn't quite fit into two suitcases apiece, so now we had to disguise a bunch of extra cargo as carry-ons, as Dad had taught us. We went to bed with huge lumps in our throats and didn't sleep much.

Early in the morning two taxis took us to the airport where we checked in at the Ecuatoriana ticket counter. Six pieces of checked baggage, including, of course, long tubes with bows and arrows and spears in them. Plus two carry-ons that a horse wouldn't have carried. Paid the airport tax, stood waiting for the boarding call.

"Ecuatoriana flight 46 to Quito and Miami is now boarding at Gate 5," said the garbled voice over the P.A. Dad wanted to pray, so we formed a circle and held hands while he led us, his voice cracking. I wonder if God was crying too.

Long hugs, but not long enough. No one could talk. We looked into each other's glistening eyes, nodded farewell and then Terry and I hoisted our bags and walked bravely to the departure gate and onto the plane. I looked out the window for waving white hands and couldn't see any, but through the mist I got a last glimpse of the Peruvian flag, waving gently in the breeze.

"Life is a Jungle!"

# Epilogue

You can take a kid out of the jungle, but it's a lot harder to take the jungle out of a kid. By the time I had been at Moody Bible Institute two years there was a new rule specifically excluding boa constrictors as dorm pets, and another rule to let students know the exact fine for getting a blowgun dart stuck in the wall.

Little did I realize as I left Peru, fearing that the rest of my life would just be like one long furlough, that I could have so much fun in the USA. Nor did I guess that I would get to go back home for some of the most exciting times of my life. Like when I joined Harriet and Hattie in their efforts to contact the Matses tribe. Or when I asked if I could help out for a summer at Yarinacocha and they made me the center director. Or when I decided to be the first one to go through the Boqueron in a rubber raft, and wasn't.

"He leadeth me, oh blessed thought." He also protecteth me, which as you will see in Book Three, was an even more blessed thought.

# SPECIAL NOTE

Although these stories may seem unusual to you, they really aren't that different from the experiences of my colleagues, my friends, my heroes.

Members of the Summer Institute of Linguistics and Wycliffe Bible Translators continue to work with minority language groups in every conceivable setting around the world, from towering mountain villages to scorching desert tents to developing cities. The pages of their lives would fill a library and are smeared with sweat, drenched in tears, underlined with laughter and overflowing with love. Their stories could be yours.

There are opportunities for service around the globe using an unbelievable variety of skills and backgrounds. If you would like more information on a most unusual way to give your life, contact Wycliffe Bible Translators USA by calling 1-800-WYCLIFFE or sending e-mail to info.usa@wycliffe.org. Or visit Wycliffe's web site at: www.wycliffe.org

P.S. If you decide to join them, start keeping good journals now. Someday, believe me, you'll want to write a book!